Sailing Through Paradise
The Illustrated Adventures of
a Single-handed Sailor

Top Cat

Sailing Through Paradise

The Illustrated Adventures of a Single-handed Sailor

by David Harris

Tortuga Books
Summerland Key, Florida

Typeface is Minion. Printed in Korea.

Publisher's Cataloguing-in-Publication
(Provided by Quality Books, Inc.)

Harris, David (David Ernest), 1942-
      Sailing through paradise : the illustrated
    adventures of a single-handed sailor / by David
    Harris. -- 1st ed.
      p. cm.
      Includes index.
      LCCN: 98-89770
      ISBN: 1-893561-01-1

      1. Harris, David (David Ernest), 1942- --
Journeys. 2. Sailing, Single-handed -- West
Indies. 3. West Indies -- Description and travel.
I. Title

F1613.H37A3 1999   910'.9163'6
                QBI99-2

For those who sail and those who dream of sea adventure — for desk-bound people everywhere

CONTENTS

5: Sailing in the Lee of Hispaniola and Crossing the Mona Passage

6: Sailing Puerto Rico's Southern Coast

7: The Spanish Virgin Islands

8: The U.S. Virgin Islands

9: Beginning My Return

10: The Big Passages

11: Sliced!

12: The Last Leg

Afterword

Index

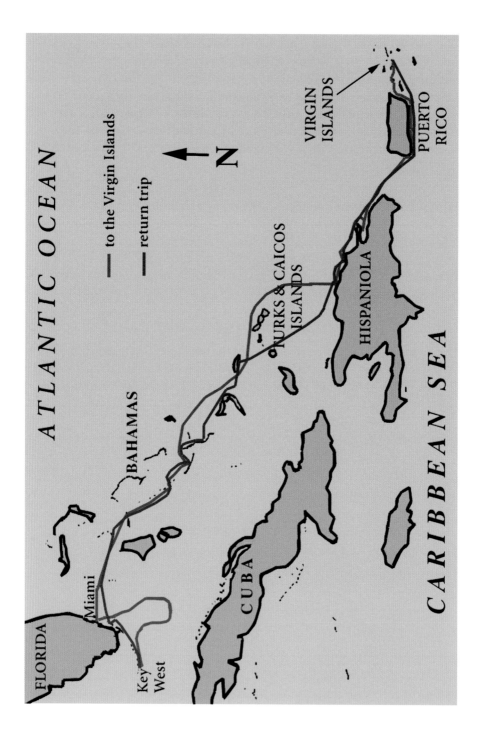

Introduction

This is the true story of my two-month trip from the Florida Keys to the Virgin Islands and back on *Top Cat*, a PDQ-32 catamaran sailboat. It is illustrated with photographs I took on the trip. My route is shown on the map on the facing page.

This book is not intended to be a cruising guide, although it may be useful to a cruiser contemplating such a trip. Many excellent cruising guides are available. Those I took on my trip are *The Gentleman's Guide to Passages South* by Bruce Van Sant (excellent for route selection), *The Yachtman's Guide to the Bahamas*, edited by Meredith Helleberg Fields (good for anchorages and piloting), *The Bahamas Cruising Guide* by Matthew Wilson (excellent information on shore-side facilities), *Reed's 1998 Caribbean Nautical Almanac* (good for tides, pilotage, and listings of radio stations), and *The 1997-98 Cruising Guide to the Virgin Islands* by Nancy and Simon Scott (good overall guide).

At age fifty-five, having just ended the last in a long series of desk-bound jobs, I felt the need for adventure, while my wife, similarly desk-bound but somewhat less daring, felt no such need. We had owned *Top Cat* for three years. The boat was manufactured in Canada by PDQ Yachts, Inc. I picked her up at the factory on Lake Ontario and, having never sailed any boat larger than a 22-foot monohull, hired a professional captain to help me take her across Ontario, through the Erie Canal, down the Hudson River to the ocean, then up the Delaware River to the Chesapeake and Delaware Canal. From there we entered Chesapeake Bay. Once we arrived at Annapolis, I felt I could handle the boat with the aid of my 11-year-old son and my wife. I paid the captain, and the three of us set off for Florida.

The trip from Annapolis to Florida was quite eventful, beginning a tradition that continues to this day. We were beset by strong currents and jellyfish in Chesapeake Bay; blinded by torrential rains as we entered Norfolk; dogged by plagues of black flies and mosquitoes. We hit a submerged tree in the Dismal Swamp Canal. Then, crossing Pamlico Sound in North Carolina, we lost an anchor and tore the sail in winds that gusted to 35 knots. Shortly thereafter, my wife flew home to attend to other business. My son and I went on.

With the sail repaired, we headed down the Intracoastal Waterway (ICW). More adventures awaited us. One morning we woke to find the boat high and dry and the water 100 feet away. Later, events conspired to push us into ground, damaging one of our two outboard engines. We left the boat at a marina for repairs and headed home by bus. My 16-year-old son and I returned, I paid the $1200 repair bill, and the two of us took the boat the rest of the way home. We left the ICW and sailed the rest of the way back to Florida on the broad blue Atlantic.

After the long trip down, we were limited to short trips as I resumed my usual position behind a desk. But I yearned for the adventure of a longer trip.

How long is long enough? How far is far enough? I settled on reaching the Caribbean Sea, much closer than the South Pacific. Would my wife come, too? After some discussion we agreed that I would sail solo to the Virgin Islands and she would fly down to join me there for a month on the boat.

I upgraded *Top Cat* for extended cruising. I added a second anchor roller, so that I could lay two anchors easily. I doubled the solar panels to provide a total of 150 watts. I bought a small SSB (single sideband) receiver, and installed a wire antenna (and a backup wire antenna) so I could pick up the offshore weather reports from the United States Coast Guard (USCG).

Fully loaded with everything I felt I needed for the trip, *Top Cat* sank about 4 inches lower in the water. I was on my way, and definitely alone. There was no room for my wife, since I had filled every empty space. I had four cameras and associated equipment, an air compressor with diving equipment, books and charts, 50 gallons of gas in a bevy of storage containers, water in containers as well as in the water tank, and food and drink for many months.

My plan was to anchor almost every night, and to travel when the weather was reasonably settled. I expected to sail at night through some passages, and now and then to sail in rough weather. I preferred this approach to a series of long passages since I tend to get seasick in bumpy seas, and don't feel good when I must go without sleep. I hoped in this way to minimize the chance of physical injury or boat damage, and increase the probability of the boat and captain arriving intact.

I...installed a wire antenna...

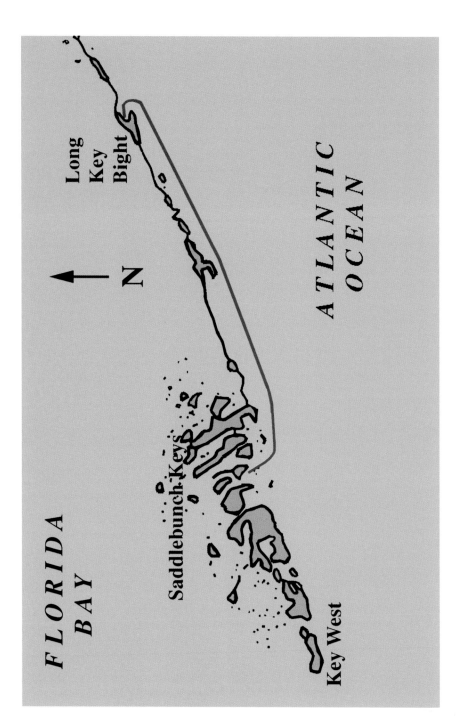

1: A Good Start

I leave from the lower keys at 7:30 in the morning on March 23. Today is the first day of spring and I am departing at high tide. I clear the channel to the sea, passing over the shoal part of it with 2 inches of water under my keel. As I head for Hawk Channel, two dolphins nose between my hulls as if to hurry me on my way. Disturbed by my approach, an anhinga bobs to the surface ahead of me and flaps away low over the water.

I leave...from the lower keys...on the first day of spring...

Once I reach Hawk Channel, I am pleased to discover I have a northwest wind. What could be better? I raise the main and roll out the jib. The water is calm, but crowded with large, expensive power yachts and strewn with endless rows of crab trap floats. I wave as the big boats pass, offering goodwill to my wealthy neighbors.

The water is ...crowded with large, expensive power yachts...

These large powerboats ignore the floats. If they hit a line, the trap and float sever their connection. While under power, *Top Cat* is vulnerable in this minefield of floats. If one of the boat's two 9.9-horsepower Yamaha outboards engages a float line, the engine quits, hopelessly entangled. I must then begin the difficult task of unsnarling the line from the propeller and shaft. Final disposition of a float often requires an impromptu swim. Today I am under sail, and floats are not so much a hazard, though I do avoid them. I have entangled one in a rudder while sailing and dragged the trap a quarter of a mile before I discovered the cause of a reduction in boat speed.

Around 4 o'clock, more than two hours before sunset, I sail north into Channel Five. Just short of the bridge I turn west into Long Key Bight, a big sheltered cove open only to the east. I lower my port engine and head into the Bight under power, dropping my main as I go. My autopilot (known more familiarly as Otto) is in charge of the helm while I tidy lines and attach the sail cover. I have had a pleasant day's sail. I hope this is a sign of things to come.

Long Key Bight is very shallow. It is a quiet anchorage unless the wind is out of the east. I anchor in 6 feet of clear water with winds now out of the west.

I raise the main...

The bottom is grassy, not particularly good for holding my anchor, but without waves or wind to worry about, I am not concerned.

At 6:30 I turn on the SSB and listen to Perfect Paul, the synthesized voice of the USCG Offshore Weather Report. While the USCG coastal reports on my VHF marine radio cover the weather in the area of my immediate interest, I feel compelled to learn to follow the SSB weather as well. The reports are content-rich, and require concentration. I resolve to hear the next one before having my drink and cooking my supper.

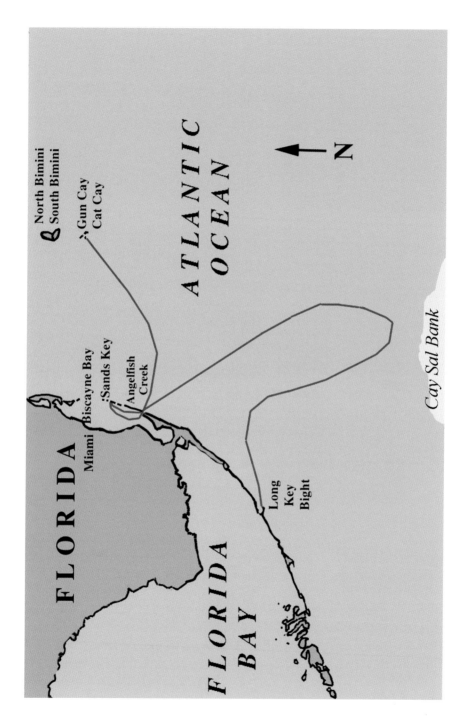

North Bimini
South Bimini
Gun Cay
Cat Cay

ATLANTIC OCEAN

N

Biscayne Bay
Sands Key
Angelfish Creek

Miami

FLORIDA

Long Key Bight

FLORIDA BAY

Cay Sal Bank

2: Crossing the Gulf Stream

Tuesday morning and the wind has shifted to the northeast at about 60 degrees and has increased to 20 knots. The wind is now coming across the only stretch of open water in the Bight! Still, we are solidly in, with little swinging in these shallow waters.

The weather does not look good. I must go northeast and the wind is from the northeast. My next destination is Cat Cay, 93 nautical miles away on a course of 65 degrees. The same distance lies between Long Key Bight and South Riding Rock, another possible destination on the other side of the Gulf Stream, at a bearing of 79 degrees. I could also go to Alice Town in North Bimini — 98 miles at 61 degrees. Every destination on the other side of the Gulf Stream requires a trip into the wind. That means no sailing, all motoring, and every mile of the trip against wind-driven waves. What to do?

I am impatient to get going. Waiting for good weather does not come easily after a lifetime of hurry-up. In my business we didn't wait, we decided on a course and took action to achieve the desired goal. Impatience is followed quickly by self-recrimination. Why am I sitting here? I should have gone last night instead of stopping for a good night's sleep. The wind was due north, and then northeast, but it was from the west when I arrived yesterday. The new forecast on VHF WX Channel 1 out of Miami for the coastal waters predicts northeast winds at 15 knots and no change in direction through Friday.

By afternoon, the wind is still blowing from the northeast, but it has dropped to about 15 knots. Tomorrow the wind will be stronger, but still from the northeast. I decide to leave right away, with the thought that if going across the Gulf Stream to Cat Cay doesn't appear to be feasible, I will head northeast up the Keys toward Miami, which will at least bring me closer to Cat Cay.

I hear small craft warnings on the weather report. *Ha!* I laugh at that. My boat is a big craft. Nevertheless, I take heed. A good rule for recreational boats is never to cross the Gulf Stream when the wind blows from the north.

The wind interacts with the 2.5-knot northward current in the Stream to produce big, chaotic waves, a messy and dangerous sea even for a big boat like
mine. Another good rule is never to go across with a wind of 20 knots or
more. I have a forecast for 15 knots of wind from the northeast, likely to
strengthen. Can I hang around Florida's coast through Friday? I may have to.

With Otto, the autopilot, in charge, I motor out of the Bight, into the wind,
with one engine. I put a single reef in the main to reduce the sail area slightly,
and hoist the sail. I turn southeast, cut the engine, unfurl the jib, and sail. It's
a little bumpy cutting across the reef line, otherwise it's not too bad.

Two hours before sunset, I arrive in the Gulf Stream a few miles off shore. I
begin to see some real waves. But I am making good time, 6 or 7 knots, bearing about 120 degrees in a comfortable reach. I don't want to push it. I am
prudent. I am just testing the waters. After an hour or two I am well on my
way. It's a beautiful evening. I see dolphins and flying fish. I compare my
speed through the water and my speed relative to the earth's surface provided
by my Global Position System (GPS) unit. Based on those data, I note that the
boost I get from the Stream toward the north seems to come and go. I have
always been dubious about our understanding of the Gulf Stream. It seems
that there are many streams, not just one.

The wind and waves begin to pick up. Big waves, and lots of spray. I have all
the hatches closed, and everything more or less put away. Since I am alone out
here, I must keep myself in as good condition as possible. I decide to take some
Dramamine before I get seasick.

I don't want to be close-hauled into this. I sail 60 degrees off the wind to get
more comfortable. My training in geometry tells me that only half of my
speed is to windward. While I am making 7 or 8 knots over the water, I am
only making 3.5 to 4 knots to windward, the direction I need to go to reach
Cat Cay. My other tack is north, and it will be fast with a strong assistance
from the Stream.

As I gaze into the dark water after nightfall, I see a host of phosphorescent
creatures sparkling in the water. They flash brightly wherever there is wave
action. I sit transfixed on the back steps, an audience of one for this marine
light show. Soon I am really bouncing, with spray everywhere. With no freighters in sight I try to rest in my starboard cabin, but before I can fall asleep,
whamp! A big wave crashes over the salon. I go out to see what can be done.

The waves are 8 to 10 feet high, commensurate with the 20-knot winds. I reef the jib. This slows us down. Six knots is better than seven when you are crashing to windward. I try not to put a lot of stress on the boat. A rogue wave smashes over the top of the boat, overwhelming the runoff channels on the hull, with the result that my salon table is drenched.

I am cold. I have put on every long-sleeved shirt I brought, and a poncho over them. The wind combined with the spray has me shivering every time I step out of the cockpit.

At about midnight I take my periodic GPS reading and discover that we are only 4 miles from Cay Sal Bank, a region of shallow water sprinkled with a few tiny islands, between Florida and Cuba. Let's head a little more north, *Top Cat*, I tell my laboring ship, or we will start this trip out with a bang. I am feeling tired, and traveling into the Bank at night is not a good idea. I change my heading. We are now on a track to Miami.

There are only two tacks. This is the good one, taking advantage of the current in the Stream. We are moving! We are also *a-bang*! and *a-slam*! as the waves smash into us. This is hard on me, hard on the boat. I try to think positively: we are making progress, doing 10 or 11 knots with 2 or 3 knots of help from the Stream.

Big waves are a work of art. I study them carefully. Most merely lift my boat, a few crash over me. There are always the rogue waves, the exceptionally large ones. These monsters tower over the boat; I look up at them as they come. They lift the boat, then we tilt down and slam into the next wave. They are all interesting, especially those with a lot of froth. After so many, they are no longer frightening. I watch them come and go. But I do worry when the boat is lifted high by one, then slammed down into the next. This puts stress on the boat, and I fear it will add to the creaks and groans in *Top Cat's* already large repertoire of noises. The north component in the wind has made the sea less organized then it would otherwise be. Waves appear to be coming from many directions.

I sail directly north on the 80-degree longitude line. By sunrise I am at 25 degrees north, approaching Miami. I need to decide now whether to set sail for the Bahamas or remain in the safety of the Keys. I am tired. We are still 50 miles from Gun Cay to the northeast. We are only 20 miles from Angelfish Creek, a direct sail at 10 knots, and the safety of Miami's Biscayne Bay. I can't get to Cat Cay directly under sail. I must tack to do that. I turn the boat to try the southwest tack, to see how bad it would be. I am headed into the current, and the waves appear bigger and badder. *Slam! Crash!* I am soaked. Every bit of the boat's exterior is wet. Everything that could fall has fallen. The boat is a mess. I decide to go to Angelfish Creek.

Morning has arrived, bringing an amazing sight. The water is full of boards. A freighter must have lost its cargo of lumber. Everywhere around me I see boards. I am glad it's daylight and I can see them and so avoid them. I watch carefully as each board goes by, perhaps 20 or 30 directly in my path. There must be hundreds of 6-foot-long boards out here.

There must be hundreds of 6-foot-long boards out here.

Going about 10 knots with a reef in the mainsail and only about 20 percent of the jib unfurled, we are really moving. It is astonishing what 20 knots of wind will do. The apparent wind — the speed of the wind plus the speed of the boat — is between 25 and 28 knots according to my wind gauge. I am enjoying a good, comfortable sail. I am so upbeat I decide to sail through Angelfish Creek without turning the motor on. While there is little wind in the creek, I come out the other side with the same 20-knot wind, but no waves to buck!

This is the life — no salt spray. Everything I touch has a rime of salt on it, especially me. I have been transformed in the course of this short journey into an old salt, or at least into an old very salty.

I enter Biscayne Bay, one of the prettiest shallow bays in the country. It is now 10 o'clock on Wednesday morning, two days after my departure, and I am still in the United States.

Near Sands Key, at one of my favorite anchorages, I stop in only 6 feet of water, protected on three sides, and listen to the howl of 20 knots of wind from the east. If the wind is bad here, the wind is really bad. There is not another boat in sight. The small craft warnings have had their effect.

I survey the boat. Standing on deck I reach up the mast as far as I can. Salt, salt everywhere.

I dinghy to shore on *Catnap*, my little hard-bottomed inflatable. I follow the narrow passageway cut through this side of Sands Key to a round, shallow pond carved out of the limestone in the island's interior.

I dinghy in to shore on Catnap...

I leave the dinghy on the shore of this little pond and follow a path east to Sands Key's Atlantic-side beach. This beach is heaped with seaweed and trash, much of it from the boats of Miamians who party in nearby waters. Apart from the trash, it is a rocky beach, tropical looking, lined with coconut palms, papaya trees, and dense brush. The sea looks calm from here.

I retrace my path out of Sands Key to ride *Catnap* on another sight-seeing trip, this one to the Boca Chica Lighthouse. The lighthouse is closed. There are no visitors today. This area is part of Key Biscayne National Park, and is usually empty except on the weekends.

...the Boca Chica Lighthouse.

This area is familiar, too familiar, the site of many previous visits. This has always been one of my favorite spots. But I can't help thinking I should be in Bimini now! I remind myself that I took the prudent course, to wait for better weather. I have no regrets.

Every week I try to run several times. I will try to do the same on this trip. Today I will run on the Elliott Key beach. Since it is a short stretch of beach, I do 25 laps to get in my 30 minutes of running. I do not meet a soul on the beach. I see nobody on the water.

The days pass slowly. Nothing to do but wait for better weather. I consume my consumables, I travel around the bay on *Catnap*, I watch boats of all kinds come and go around me. My camera provides me with something to do. I take pictures of other boats, the sea, the sky, birds poking through the shallow waters around these tiny keys.

...birds poking through the shallow waters...

Thursday, Friday, Saturday…

By Sunday the wind has weakened enough for me to make a second attempt to cross the Gulf Stream. I leave about 3 o'clock in the afternoon for a sail down Biscayne Bay to Angelfish Creek. The bay is full of Miamians out for a good time. I pass Sands Cut, with dozens of boats pushed up on the sand in shallow water so their passengers can splash about and socialize. Farther south I pass the Elliott Key beach, also full of people. As I sail through Cutter Cut, a narrow channel through the shallows that separate Biscayne Bay from Card Sound, five large powerboats come through. The operators slow down, allowing me to proceed without having to climb and descend mountains of wake. Sail has its perks (as implemented by international boating law).

I prepare to turn to port into Angelfish Creek and attempt to disengage my autopilot, but it won't disengage! Otto clings stubbornly to the helm. He is in control and won't let go.

This is not the first time Otto has done this. The last time was on a family trip, approaching Tarpon Springs on Florida's west coast. I dealt with it then by detaching the control ring from the wheel (a matter of removing three bolts). Each time we used the autopilot after that, I had to reattach the control ring. When we wanted to disengage, I'd remove the bolts. This went on for the rest of the trip and proved to be a real inconvenience. It took much of the "auto" out of "autopilot." The system was eventually fixed, under warranty, by the manufacturer. Since then I have kept the Allen wrench I use to remove the bolts near at hand on the salon table. A good thing, too, because I need it now.

I remove the autopilot, regaining control of the boat, and look for a place to anchor so I can investigate Otto's problem. I choose Peanut Key, about a mile away. As I round the island I see a group of sailboats anchored, so I pick a spot near them. After I am anchored I look carefully at the autopilot and discover that the lever that engaged and disengaged the unit has broken. Good news! Maybe I can fix it.

I locate my visegrips and replace the broken lever. It works! I can engage and disengage the autopilot. I lift anchor and depart.

By now the sun has set, and it is dark, so I must make my way through Angelfish Creek at night, and a very dark night it is. I motor through, using my binoculars to locate the unlighted channel markers. With the aid of *Top Cat's* GPS, and my now-functional autopilot, I am soon back in the Gulf Stream for a second shot at crossing to Cat Cay. I have no wish to motor into 15-knot east winds, so I again sail southeast across the Stream. Travel is easier this time, with smaller waves and quieter winds. At 8 o'clock I warm up a can of stew. It's going to be a long night.

I pass three large cruise ships moving south. They are only 15 minutes apart, apparently all out of Miami in late afternoon. They are lit up like small cities, lights everywhere, and the closer I get the more the detail I can see. Later I pass several tankers. I avoid, with small course changes, getting close to any of these big ships. By morning I am nearing the Great Bahama Bank, about 20 miles south of Cat Cay. I tack, turning the boat through the wind to head north, and begin to move much more quickly.

At noon I arrive at Cat Cay. I have been awake for about 30 hours, and I have seen quite a bit of the Stream. Nice, but I think I have had enough. I take

The megayacht ...leaves a wake that reminds me of the Stream.

down the sails, put lines on each corner, bumpers out, yellow quarantine flag up to show I am a new arrival and must clear customs, and head for port. The megayacht leaving port as I motor in leaves a wake that reminds me of the Stream.

As I swing into port I call the harbormaster on my VHF radio and request directions for clearing customs. This place looks like big money. The Bahamian workers ride around in golf carts. I have trouble at first understanding the harbormaster. Where does he want me to go? Suddenly, my starboard engine dies. I try to restart it. No luck. Is my battery gone? I switch to the other battery, and the engine starts, but it doesn't sound right. I make it in to the harbor, drifting into the end of the dock. A marina worker comes out to help me tie up.

I seem to have lost control of the boat with the engines on. What's wrong? I see the problem. I left a line on the trampoline — the netting bridge between hulls that serves *Top Cat* as a front deck — and the line fell overboard probably while I was motoring past the big yacht. It is tangled in the starboard engine propeller. I manage to work the line out of its entanglement but I am too tired to think about possible damage to the engine.

I am delayed while the customs officer lunches, then while he drives a friend to the airport. The island is small. I can easily see the airport, and one small plane. As promised, fifteen minutes after the plane departs the customs officer arrives to clear me. I have been waiting about 90 minutes for a five-minute transaction. (Patience! I tell myself.)

He appears to enjoy his job. He has a radio and is listening to music. Bahamian officials are almost always pleasant and efficient, and I feel comfortable dealing with them. Workers here carry VHF radios, and constantly use them to carry on long conversations. As I wait I watch them talk to people sometimes just 50 feet away.

Finally finished with customs, I find I am exhausted. I back the boat up, and try to turn around. The boat simply will not respond. I drift to shallows, and am soon aground. I get myself out using a long pole kept on the deck for just this purpose. I realize suddenly that the starboard engine was hosed by its encounter with the line that fell overboard. I leave for the nearest anchorage under port engine power.

I anchor, too tired to do anything about my starboard engine problem.   I am on the east side of Gun Cay. There are eleven sailboats anchored on the west side, downwind, and none on the east side. I have been here before, however, and I am not concerned about my choice. Once squared away for the night, I collapse, sleeping 12 hours straight.

Tuesday dawns. It's time to take care of the outboard motor. I spend six hours pulling the engine out of the water, up onto the deck. I determine that the slip clutch on the propeller is damaged. In the process of changing the propeller, I nearly lose a metal piece that holds the controls onto the engine, something I have done before. Once, the engine itself nearly slips into the sea. I cut myself several times. And all of this, *all*, because a line fell overboard! For the umpteenth time, I miss my wife. If she were here she would have handled the line as I approached the dock; there would have been no need for me to set out the lines before entering the harbor.

At least my problem with the engine has not caused a delay. Conditions are no good for sailing anyway. A 20-knot wind is blowing from the southeast, too much wind for me. I notice that the sailboats that were on the west side of Cat Cay have moved around to Honeymoon Harbor. The west-side anchorage has a bad ocean swell, making for an uncomfortable stay.

Honeymoon Harbor is beautiful, but small.

Honeymoon Harbor is beautiful, but small. It's a cramped anchorage, and with the remains of dead boats along its beaches, it is also a rather ominous environment for a sailboat.

During my last visit here on a trip with my wife, we passed a large sailboat firmly stuck in the sand. The owner needed help pulling her out, but our two little outboards didn't have the power to budge her, so we didn't even offer to try. I dinghied over to lend the captain a hand putting out his anchor so the waves wouldn't push the boat any farther toward shore. He said that unless he could get his sailboat off, he would have to pay $10,000 for a towboat from Fort Lauderdale. He explained that he and his wife had left their boat to have lunch at Cat Cay. When they returned, it was aground. He seemed very disheartened by his experience, and was contemplating selling his boat. The next morning, very early, we heard the towboat, and when we got up, the sailboat was gone, presumably on a very expensive return trip to Florida.

I dinghy over to the beach and talk with a man who owns a trimaran anchored in the harbor. He says he is trying to make it to Nassau to meet a plane on Saturday. He tells me that a boat was pulled off the reef at the entrance to Honeymoon Harbor two days ago. I tell him of our experience with the sailboat the previous year. It is easy to drag an anchor since the bottom is generally poor holding here and the current is fairly strong.

He has a cockleshell dinghy...

I walk over to the other side of Gun Cay, trying to decide whether I should run. There isn't much beach, and a run would require a lot of backing-and-forthing. I meet a man, a solo sailor like me, walking the beach. He looks like a tattooed version of Popeye, only smaller and tougher. He has a cockleshell dingy — no fancy inflatable contraptions for him. I can tell he marches to the beat of a different drummer.

I always pull the dinghy far up the beach when I leave it, but this time I have not pulled it far enough. When I return, in less than fifteen minutes, *Catnap* is adrift in the middle of Honeymoon Harbor. I dive into the water to swim to retrieve it, and am most of the way over to it when a snorkeler, the trimaran owner, gets there first and grabs it for me.

I awake Wednesday morning with 18 knots of wind from the southeast. I decide to stay another day. Weaker winds are surely on their way. By noon all the original boats are gone, but new ones have arrived. In the afternoon the wind drops to 8 knots. Powerboats begin showing up.

I dinghy over to Honeymoon Harbor and talk to some powerboaters. They have come over this morning, the first good boating day in a long time. Powerboats usually come with many people, while most sailboats carry a husband and wife, which illustrates perfectly the nature of travel aboard each kind of craft. A big group is comfortable covering the long distance between the U.S. mainland and the Bahamas on a powerboat; the trip only takes a few hours. For a sailboat's much slower journey, everyone will need a place to sleep, and several days of meals will be required for the trip over and back.

One group of six off a powerboat is down from Long Island, New York. They look sunburned already, on their first day in the Bahamas. I take their pictures in front of their boat with their camera. They will have this photographic remembrance of their trip and doubtless will tell stories about meeting me, just as I am telling here about meeting them.

During my late-afternoon run up and down Gun Cay I count the wrecked boats. It is hard, since boat parts are everywhere. Does that group of parts belong to one boat, or to two? I eventually settle on five. There are five distinctly different wrecks, five dead boats, along my path.

I spend the afternoon watching the birds and climbing over the rocks along the shoreline. The sea continues to be rough.

I spend the afternoon watching the birds and climbing over the rocks...

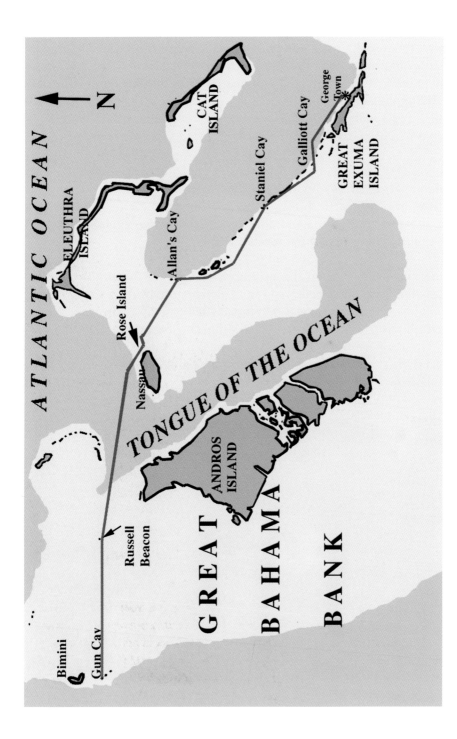

3: Crossing the Great Bahama Bank

I leave early on Thursday morning, April 2, heading for Russell Beacon, about 45 miles away in the middle of the Great Bahama Bank. Conditions are good, with light winds from the southeast. I sail with an assist from the starboard engine. As I leave, I see a sailboat hard aground off Cat Cay about two miles away. The tide is rising, so for this craft there is hope of escape.

The Bank amazes me...

The Bank amazes me — a patch of shallow water thousands of square miles in area in the middle of the sea! There is nothing out here. The bottom is sandy, with occasional patches of grass. I see no coral heads. No fish. One dolphin. One Portuguese man-o-war. After a while I lose interest in watching for coral heads, since I haven't seen even one. I decide I am safe from collision with a coral head and resign from head watch. I get busy polishing *Top Cat's* brightwork.

Out here, the boats are the main event. One looks like a pirate ship, with gaff rigging. It heads directly for me. I reach for my musket. The pirate ship is near enough now for me to make out the evil grins of bloodthirsty, coldhearted, sword-wielding buccaneers. — Fortunately, it is not a pirate ship, which is good because I have forgotten to bring my musket. The captain waves. I wave back. Most of the boats that I see are powerboats, some small, some large. They all pass me on this 60-mile-long water highway. I am the slowest thing on the road.

Fortunately, it is not a pirate ship...

Ahead I see water that is much lighter in color than the rest. Could it be shallow? I slow to enter this region, looking carefully for trouble, but soon determine that the water is cloudy, not shallow. Right up to its edge I see the bottom clearly at 15 feet. Then all visibility is lost. The water is churned up, and what I am seeing is a slurry of sand and water. I cannot even see my rudders a few feet below the surface. In under a mile we break through into clear water again.

I arrive near Russell Beacon about 4:30. For the first time, I set two anchors, one up-current and one down-current. Then, dutifully, I dive on each anchor to ensure that they are properly set. The task is harder here, since I am in 20 feet of water. The anchors look fine. I see grass below me, but no fish.

I am truly off in the middle of nowhere, out in the Great Bahama Bank. It does give me a start! I put on two anchor lights as it gets dark, a bright one on the top of my mast, a dimmer one partway down. I can be seen by ships near and far. Nobody who is watching out will bump into me in the middle of the night. I am a mile from Russell Beacon. Russell Beacon, which should be lit, is dark tonight.

While I am first to stop, by 8 o'clock seven boats are clustered around me. The idea seems to be that there is safety in numbers. Bahamian mailboats come through here at night, and they could ram right into one of us if they are not paying attention.

I soon learn why anchoring on the banks in open water is a bad idea. First, there is always a strong current due to tide. As the bulge of water created by the moon's tidal pull runs over this shallow ocean plateau, the water, forced through a smaller space, begins to flow very rapidly. So much water trying to move over such a shallow area results in a very strong current. Second, and most important, the direction of the wind is independent of the current. For me this means that, while *Top Cat* is anchored to align with the current, the wind-driven waves are hitting us abeam. The boat is therefore in constant motion as the tide pulls it one way and the wind catches it and pushes it back the other way. Rock and roll, all night long. By midnight there is some serious wallowing going on. I wedge myself into my bunk to avoid being thrown onto the floor.

I keep hearing all sorts of noises. — Creaking boat sounds from the interior and metallic clanging sounds from the rudder.

Creaking I know. It is familiar and does not concern me. The clanging sounds, however, galvanize me into action. I leap from my bunk and hurry outside to examine the steering system. I take everything out of the aft lockers and crawl below. Is something loose? No.

Having failed to find the problem, I return to bed, but cannot get to sleep. Later I discover that by pushing hard on the rudder, I can make the cylinder connecting the two rudders inside the boat ring. The periodic force of the current on the rudder as the wind swings the boat creates this same effect.

In the morning I am up at daybreak, but still I am the last to leave. All the other boats are gone. It looks like nobody had a good night and they all left as soon as they could. I head to the Northwest Channel light, about 15 miles away. I sail with motor on, intent on getting off the Bank as soon as possible. More boats pass, including a ferry from the Abacos.

Soon I am at the Northwest Channel light, or what remains of it. It looks as if it has sustained some damage, perhaps a collision or two, and resembles a piece of wreckage in the sea. I head out into the Northwest Channel to Nassau. The Northwest Channel cuts across the north end of the Tongue of the Ocean. In this area the water is quite deep, between one and two miles. The Tongue extends about a hundred miles south of me. I will meet up with the Great Bahama Bank again when I reach Nassau, my next destination.

The wind is weak and from the southwest. I keep the sails up and an engine on. I want to make my anchorage before dark. I keep three anchorage options open, one in Nassau Harbor (the closest), one behind Salt Cay (easiest to enter), and one at Bottom Harbor behind Rose Island. Nassau Harbor is not a quiet place to anchor because of heavy boat traffic. It is last on my list of options. Salt Cay is open to the south, the current direction of the wind, so is apt to be somewhat bumpy.

During the long trip I watch the boat traffic, do the dishes, and clean the boat's interior. To preserve my water supply, I wash dishes in saltwater, sometimes in a bucket in the cockpit when underway, sometimes in the galley sink when the boat is quiet. Dawn liquid dish detergent works well, and if the dishes are rinsed in saltwater and immediately dried, there is no salt residue.

I listen to the U.S. National Weather Service report on my VHF radio, on Channel WX 1 out of Miami. The weather report from Miami, of course, only predicts conditions in south Florida coastal waters.

I arrive at Bottom Harbor at sunset, for a total of 63 miles traveled today. The seas are getting rougher and the wind blows at 20 knots. The small harbor is filled with boats. I must anchor before total darkness. It is about an hour from low tide, and I am in four-foot water, wondering if I can find a place with enough water to keep me afloat all night. I cut the engines and drop one an-

I wash dishes...in a bucket in the cockpit...

chor, then dinghy out with a second anchor and dump it overboard. *Top Cat* drifts back into five feet of water with two anchors out. It is dark, too late to dive on the anchors. I am surrounded by rocky outcroppings on three sides. Each anchor carries about 40 feet of chain. I have a scope of about 10. (The scope is the ratio of length of the anchor rode to the height of bow above the bottom.) I feel secure.

It is a bouncy and sleepless night again, and I leave early in the morning as a weak front begins to pass. I motor west along the craggy rocks of Rose Island, pass the entrance to the saltpans, then go south. The wind is out of the south, at about 18 knots. Once south of Porgee Rock Light I put up the sails with a reef in the main, cut the engine, and head out across the Great Bahama Bank again, this time for the Exuma Cays, a 150-mile chain of hundreds of islands.

I must cross part of the Yellow Bank, an area dotted with coral heads according to the chart. I wonder how easily I can spot them in this rough water. By 10 o'clock I have arrived at the Yellow Bank, so I climb up to sit on the hardtop that covers the cockpit, a perch that provides me with an excellent view at about 8 feet above the water. A moment after I am in position, we hit a large wave and I am drenched. Undaunted, I remain at my post to stand watch. I see some really dark areas (coral heads, I assume) easily, and steer around them. A yacht nearby is doing the same thing, but the yacht is going a different direction and has sunlight from behind, making the job easy.

I stop at 1:30 near Allan's Cay to disassemble Otto, and I take down the sails. I turn on both engines to enter the harbor in 20-knot winds and very bouncy seas. Four boats are already anchored in the harbor, but there is a spot for me. This is the advantage of stopping early: it's first come, first served, as far as anchorage space is concerned. Again I put down two anchors. According to the forecast, the wind will clock from south through southwest to north.

The bottom is good, deep sand, but I dive on the anchors anyway, in part, admittedly, because I feel like a swim. A small stingray glides by, dogged by a fish of equal length, about a foot and a half. Another fish swims alongside. The stingray is obviously annoyed, and zigzagging to escape from these escorts. Rays and skates seem to be everywhere on the bank. They are dark and stand out well against the light sand bottom.

Leaf Cay is teeming with iguanas.

I dinghy to Leaf Cay, to the east of Allan's Cay. Leaf Cay is teeming with iguanas. They rush at me as I stroll across the beach, a rather unnerving experience. Leaf Cay smells like a chicken house — it must be the iguanas. A sign on the beach claims that these cays are unique as a last home for these endangered reptiles. Each iguana is marked on its back with either blue or red paint. I assume the marks indicate their sex. I certainly can't tell whether they are male or female by looking.

Each iguana is marked on its back with either blue or red paint.

It is upscale graffiti, with no dirty words.

Above the beach on the hill stands a decaying building covered with yachtie graffiti. It is upscale graffiti, with no dirty words.

Soon I learn why the iguanas stampeded toward me when I hit the beach. A boat from Nassau arrives with scores of tourists. The guide hops off and begins to throw what looks like bread to the reptiles. The iguanas wolf down

these offerings while the tourists watch, entranced: chow time for the endangered reptiles, a photo op for the tourists.

Tourists and iguanas scramble...for fun and food all over the beach.

I head for the cay to the south in my dinghy where a Bahamian fishing boat
passes. For a while I have it to myself. Soon, too soon, two boats of tourists
arrive. Tourists and iguanas scramble in a mad dash for fun and food all over
the beach.

I retreat to the cay on the west, where I see more birds than iguanas. The west
side is open to the weather, and is very rocky. The birds are noisy but for some
reason I am unable to see them. While most seem to stay hidden in the bushes,
I get a picture of one as he briefly sits on top of a bush ahead of me, and I take
other pictures, some of flowers, some of the rocky shoreline, and several of a
friendly bird I identify later as a ruddy turnstone. This island doesn't smell so
much like iguanas as the other two, but I see iguanas here.

Back to the boat for a drink and supper, and then to bed. Will I be able to
leave tomorrow?

The wind is still strong on Sunday morning, so I decide to stay. I take up the
anchors and motor in *Top Cat* to the east side of Leaf Cay, where there are

...I take ...pictures...of a friendly bird...

fewer iguanas and perhaps less boat traffic. I dinghy to shore and accomplish my 30-minute run by running back and forth about twenty times. A group arrives a few minutes after I do. They are locals, they say, from Nassau, but seem very British to me. I complete my run, and return to the boat for a swim to check the anchors.

Today marks the end of two weeks at sea. My supplies, for the most part, are holding up well. I finished my bananas in the first week, and the oranges today. I have plenty of apples left, all in good condition. I keep the fruit out of the light, under a towel. I have just finished the bread and the sandwich meat. Although I have been taking a light shower every night, I have used only half of the water in my 10-gallon shower bag. The bag stays on deck, absorbing the warmth of the sun, and provides a warm shower after I swim to check the anchors each night. About 40 percent of my gas is gone, but I estimate most of the water in my main tank remains. I have hardly made a dent in the canned food or canned drink supplies. And, most importantly, the limes I brought from our tree in the Keys (to flavor my gin-and-tonics) are holding up well.

I have quite a variety of canned and dried foods on board. One of my favorite dinners is Minute Rice with a meat sauce I make from a can of turkey and a can of Campbell's Mushroom Soup. I also have a huge supply of pasta and pasta sauce. I brought cans of salmon, tuna and sardines. I produce instant dinners from cans of stew, chicken with dumplings, beef chow mein, ravioli, spaghetti, chili, and chicken with rice. In addition to a full range of canned vegetables, I have several varieties of canned bean and potato salads. I have canned and dried fruits, nuts, crackers, snacks and candies. I have boxes of milk and cereal for breakfast, and many cases of soft drinks and bottles of seltzer and spring water. *Top Cat* is a floating grocery store.

Many of the boats that were here when I arrived are now gone. Some only passed through the harbor, not anchoring, perhaps because there are too many boats. A big catamaran did that, greatly to my regret, since I would like to have had company, and a closer look at it. Now there are several large powerboats here with *Top Cat*. One, *Let It Be*, is much larger than the others, possibly 70 feet long or more. All the powerboats are bigger than the sailboats here, and clearly much more expensive. They all carry boatloads of people to the shore to see the iguanas. *Let It Be* has a tender piloted by a small boy that seems to shuttle back and forth continuously.

...a tender piloted by a small boy...

By sunset I am convinced I will probably leave in the morning, so I take a trip to the west side of Leaf Cay for a walk with my gin-and-tonic. There are few iguanas on the west side, I suppose because the tourists always come to the east side. It is very peaceful, and I come back relaxed.

I am surprised on my return to see *Top Cat* facing northeast while all the other boats face southwest to northwest. What's up? Current and wind are at odds, as usual. The wind is weakening, and no long dominates the direction boats face. I wonder how many times my boat will wrap itself around the anchor tonight. — This calls for another drink.

The weather report at 6:15 the next morning on Nassau radio (1540 AM) is favorable. Perfect Paul (the USCG offshore weather report, delivered by synthesized voice on SSB) has not so much as a discouraging word for me. The Nassau radio weather report appears to cover the area around and south of Nassau well. The National Weather Service Offshore Report for the Southwest North Atlantic delivered by the USCG covers weather over the open water. There is never a reference to land masses, only to positions in latitude and longitude. The report is limited to a sentence or two when the weather is generally favorable, as it is today. Time to go!

Surprise! The anchor lines are not tangled! I pull them up easily and motor out heading southeast. I raise the sail and reassemble the autopilot when I reach open water. It's a good sail with a calm sea despite days of strong wind. When the wind returns to the east, the water over the Bank settles down quickly.

I arrive at Big Major's Spot near Staniel Cay at 4 o'clock, anchor, and immediately leave by dinghy for Thunderball Cave. I can't miss seeing the place where my favorite movie hero James Bond chased the bad guys in "Thunderball"! I arrive at the cave at precisely the same time as a group from *Let It Be*, small boys included. The skiff disgorges divers in full scuba gear who quickly disap-

...Thunderball Cave...

pear inside the cave. After mooring my dinghy, I jump into the water with fins and snorkel, clutching my underwater camera in the hope of taking some good pictures of the cave. The cave entrance is guarded by hundreds of small, colorful fish. The current is tremendous; there is no way I can enter the cave and live to tell about it. I decide to retreat. I tour the area by dinghy, stopping to take pictures of the wreck of a large fishing boat on the beach.

...the wreck of a large fishing boat...

Next, I head over to see the cut to Exuma Sound, and to look at Club Thunderball. The current in and out of Big Rock Cut appears to be very strong and I decide not to take my dinghy through. Instead, I tour Staniel Cay where there is a marina surrounded by colorful Bahamian houses. I spot a large catamaran off the settlement. I have become a bit of an expert on catamarans, having researched the purchase of *Top Cat* for nearly a year and attended various boat shows, and I am always interested when I see one.

I return to *Top Cat* to discover that a megayacht, *La Belle*, a craft even bigger than *Let It Be*, has anchored right next to me. The boat is full of partying people, perhaps twenty or more. I wonder if they have seen Thunderball Cave.

...colorful Bahamian houses.

Tuesday morning, April 7, I manage to leave the harbor without bumping *La Belle*. I leave under sail and pass in front of the yacht, slightly raising the chance of collision. I notice several crew members cleaning the ship's brightwork and mopping the deck. (I have never mopped my deck!) I see no guests out on deck this early. Partying is hard work and requires plenty of sleep.

I sail south toward Galliot Cut. That's where I plan to leave the banks, weather permitting. The sail is close-hauled, as close to the wind as I can get, about 45 degrees from the direction of the apparent wind. This tack is bumpy, and travel is slow. Catamarans like *Top Cat* are much faster in a beam reach, about 90 degrees from the wind. As I approach Galliot Cay, the water begins to get thinner and starts to look like water around the Florida Keys. The depth here is only about 8 feet. The water takes on the green hue typical in the Keys on the Gulf side, though there are no crab traps here, as there are in the shallow waters around the Keys. I see more sand here, and less mud and grass.

 The biggest difference to me now is that these are mainly uncharted and un-marked waters; the waters around the Florida Keys, like all U.S. waters, are completely charted and marked with an extensive and reliable buoy system. I will have to watch out or I will end up aground.

As I turn toward Galliot Cay I notice an enormous sandbar to the south and wonder if it would be a good place to run. I anchor in a hurry off Galliot Cay and dinghy out to the bar while it is still low tide. As I arrive at the bar, another dinghy leaves. The tide is coming in fast, so I drag the dinghy as far up the sand as I can. The beach is miles long, and is indeed a great beach for running. I jog down a mile or so, then back to the boat, then back down the beach. I see the water coming in, and know that soon my jogging beach will disappear from under my feet. I put in my 35 minutes running, and return with dry feet to the dinghy. I take a few pictures before I go.

...a great beach for running.

After the run I cruise the islands. There are caves everywhere, as well as beautiful beaches. I walk several of these beaches, all empty. I see many thatch palms, miniature palm trees like those in the Keys. One has a bullet hole through it. I climb to the top of Galliot Cay, and marvel at the ferocious waves in Exuma Sound. Will I really leave through that tomorrow? Arriving back at the boat, I dive on the anchors; all is well.

The weather does not look good in the morning, but I decide to go anyway. The winds are 15 to 20 knots from the east to southeast, with more of the same predicted for the next day, and Friday even worse as a front moves down from Georgia. I motor through Galliot Cut and into a very rough Exuma Sound. The cut is particularly bumpy, and one errant wave drenches me as I sit at the wheel. The cut appears deep to me, at least 20 feet, although it is described in my guidebooks as shallow. Once out at sea, I reassemble the autopilot and put Otto in charge of the helm. I dress in dry clothing and put on my heavy-weather suit.

The seas are so rough that one of my 9.9-horsepower Yamahas is insufficient to make much headway. I need two roaring engines. I will consume twice the fuel, over a gallon per hour for the estimated seven-hour trip to George Town. As I calculate the cost implications of my situation, it occurs to me why I have seen so few medium-sized powerboats in the south Exumas, though they are numerous around Nassau. With a 300-horsepower powerboat consuming 20 or 30 gallons per hour (a range of 1/2 to 1 gallon per hour for each 10 horse-power is typical for gas engines) a ten-hour round trip from Nassau would cost about $750 at current Bahamian gas prices. (Gas prices here are between two and three times the typical cost in Florida.) The really rich in the megayachts don't care about the cost of fuel; the rest come in sailboats. Those who own medium-sized powerboats have less money for gas and don't venture this far south.

Driving into the waves results in a wet trip. Worse, the boat is so bouncy that reading a book is impossible. I sit and watch the ocean as Otto steers.

Soon I am nearing Great Exuma Island, and George Town. I follow the zigzag course outlined in the guides and the Bahamas Chart Kit for the entry into Elizabeth Harbour. I let Otto handle the controls so that I can concentrate on the landmarks, and check my GPS waypoints. I steer to six waypoints coming in, taking a very conservative course. Following my waypoints, the course headings given by Fields in *The Yachtsman's Guide to the Bahamas* for each turn come out perfectly.

Sailboats are all around me as I near George Town. It is April 8. The Family Island Regatta is held here in mid-April, attracting hundreds of boats. In addition, a large contingent of cruisers stay permanently in George Town, living on their boats moored in the harbor. There are probably over 200 boats here now, but there is clearly room for many more. This is a very large harbor.

Sailboats are all around me...

I anchor in sand off Regatta Point, putting out two anchors. I am becoming an expert now at two anchors and have evolved a much simpler system than I used at Russell Beacon. One complicating issue for me is that a catamaran should have a bridle for each anchor. (A bridle is a line attached to each bow of a catamaran to which a second line, the rode of the anchor in this case, can be attached.)

With one anchor this is simple. I use a single line from the anchor rode to the opposite bow to ensure that the anchor pulls on both bows. At Russell Beacon I used a bridle that connected to each bow, then from a loop in the middle to each rode. This was hard to connect if I first drifted back on one anchor, laid the second anchor, then pulled back up to a shorter rode on the first anchor. My latest procedure is to begin by anchoring normally with the first anchor. Then, using my dinghy, I ferry the second anchor first to a point in front of *Top Cat* to attach a short line connecting the two rodes, and then take it out and drop it overboard. Back on *Top Cat* I can adjust the anchor rodes to achieve a perfect bridle whether the boat is held by one anchor or the other. The bridle will now consist of the downstream anchor rode and the short connecting line on one side, and the upstream anchor rode on the other.

After a dive on the anchors and a quick shower, I dinghy in. There are several dinghy docks on Lake Victoria, which is connected to the harbor by a short channel. Dinghies are everywhere, and they are generally not locked. I leave my dinghy among many that are similar. One, in fact, is identical to mine.

This small town appears to accommodate the cruising yachtie. The market has a full line of supplies, all relatively expensive. I buy sandwich meat and tomatoes at the Exuma Markets, a small, air-conditioned grocery store much like those back home in the Keys. I pick up two loaves of bread from Mom at Mom's Bakery, which is actually a van turned into a store. She bakes her breads at home and brings them to town to sell them from her van. Mom is a very warm person and greets most customers with a hug, but I manage to avoid her embrace. Her breads are great, $2.50 per loaf.

There are also vegetable markets, a bank, a UPS office, a laundramat, a liquor store, restaurants and a government building. I think there is more civilization here than I need. I use the laundramat located across the lake in a large pink building on a hill. A Bahamian lady and I are the only people in the place. The machines appear to be identical to laundramat machines I serviced as a high school student in the late 1950s. I know where to put the U.S.

quarters. U.S. and Bahamian money are totally interchangeable, although I observe that while I nearly always pay in U.S. currency, I get Bahamian dollars in change.

I fill up with fuel, but skip the water available on the dinghy docks. I discuss water quality with two cruisers. One says yes, you can drink it. The other says no, you shouldn't. I am sure even as I pass it up that I will come to regret leaving without water. The fuel, at $2.71 per gallon, is only slightly more expensive than a $1.80 gallon container of drinking water available in the Exuma

I think there is more civilization here than I need.

Markets. I pump the fuel from the shore pump into my 6-gallon containers, then carry them to my dinghy. Fuel is clearly more important to me than drinking water.

Cruisers have many traditions. One is to greet each new cruiser on arrival. They contact arriving boats by VHF radio in George Town; one is expected to monitor Channel 16 at all times. When I first came into port I turned off my radio even before I dropped anchor. Two cruisers came by to admonish me about this, since I was unreachable, exactly what I had in mind. I wanted peace and quiet — and a nap. The VHF radio is like the old party-line telephones in that you can listen in on every conversation. A cruiser is hailed on Channel 16 and then, if a connection is made to the right party, both switch to another channel to talk. I spend some time listening to the constant chatter. Get-togethers are arranged, problems are discussed, and gossip is traded.

I am invited over for drinks and snacks at a nearby boat. I enjoy the company of two cruising couples, and receive their cards. The cards, like business cards, identify the cruisers, their boat, and their mailing address. I decide that I will bring cards like theirs on my next trip. Many cruisers, I believe, are anchored here for life.

I phone my wife. I tell her I bought her a basket at a little street market in George Town. She tells me she has ordered a new autopilot, and has had it sent to me here on Great Exuma Island. Today is Thursday, and tomorrow is Good Friday. The next mail boat comes in on Wednesday, after the four-day holiday. Nothing happens in Nassau either, during the four-day holiday, and all mail goes through Nassau. So my guess is that a three-day package will arrive on Thursday or Friday of next week, too long a wait for me. I will not wait for it. In fact, I should have left this morning. The weather has been perfect for the next leg of my voyage, my trip to Rum Cay.

It is 7 o'clock and the wind is very light, from the south. The gulls are squawk-ing. I am anchored on dredged ground, nothing but sand. Much of the Eliza-beth Harbor was dredged when this was a U.S. Navy base in World War II. Tomorrow will be a day full of events here in George Town, with roster sheets everywhere for yachties and Bahamians to sign up for the regatta. Next week is the annual Bahamian regatta. Last month they held the annual regatta for cruisers. This is Regatta Central.

A front is coming through, providing a good opportunity for me to move southeast. When the tradewinds from the east are disrupted by a front, a sailboat can travel southeast under sail, my direction to the Virgin Islands, with some degree of comfort. I have just finished motoring into the southeast tradewinds on my trip from Galliot Cut to George Town. I will avoid doing it again soon if I can.

...I bought her a basket at a little street market in George Town.

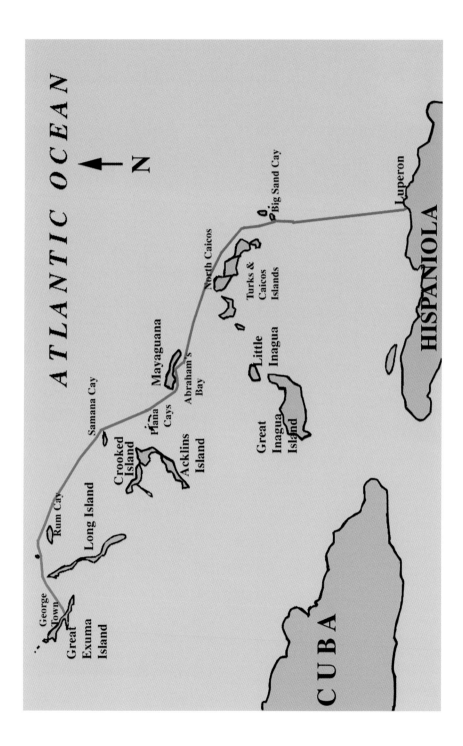

4: Navigating the Southwest North Atlantic

At daybreak I leave from Regatta Point. It takes me almost an hour to leave George Town, with the final 15 minutes on a careful watch for heads. It is early, so spotting heads is tougher than usual. I take a route that does not go directly into the rising sun, but still the light interferes with my view into the water.

The wind is out of the south. Later, according to the forecast, it will move to the southwest, then quickly to the northwest as the front passes, and finally back to east. I plan to get as far as I can before the wind turns back to east.

I sail past Cape Santa Maria early in the morning, out of Exuma Sound and into the Southwest North Atlantic. Except for a small Bahamian boat near the Cape, I am alone. I stay ahead of the front. I think it must be moving slowly. The winds remain consistently out of the south, and in the 10- to 15-knot range, for a pleasant sail.

Once in the open Atlantic, I sail for Rum Cay. As I close on it sailing southeast, the wind continues from the south. The weather reports confirm my impression that the front is a slow-moving one, and I am well out ahead of it. *Yes!* I am pleased with my progress and delighted by the prospect of a long, comfortable sail.

I continue sailing past Rum Cay, toward Samana Cay, and into the tropics. The tropics begin officially at the Tropic of Cancer, latitude 23 degrees, 26 minutes. The words "tropic" and "tropical" are used with little concern for precise meaning in Florida. For example, though we are over a degree north of the Tropic of Cancer where we live in the Keys, local radio stations freely employ the adjective "tropical" in their promotions and ads. Now I am well and truly in the topics, but despite the location, I am still wearing a long-sleeved shirt. So far, this has been a cold trip.

The weather forecasts predict south to southwest winds through tonight, although it is not clear to me when the front will catch me. I decide to skip Samana Cay and head farther southeast to the Plana Cays. I sail through the night, but preserve my rituals. I have my drink at 6 o'clock, dinner at 7. I watch the sun set. At 8, I listen to my shortwave radio. I have plenty of channels to choose from at night, when the reception is best. I listen to a show on Liberian child soldiers from Radio Netherlands, news from the British Broadcasting Corporation (BBC), then news from the Voice of America (VOA), broadcast in very basic English. I am getting tired. I see not a single boat all night, but make steady progress. By morning I am off the Plana Cays, two uninhabited sandy islands with reefs to the north.

I round East Plana in early morning, and head for Mayaguana. The Plana Cays are not a good place to stop in southwest winds, and I have southwest winds. I'll use them before I lose them. Shortly after lunch, I approach Mayaguana. I am exhausted. I feel I can go no farther. As I round Devil's Point at the western end of Mayaguana headed toward Abraham's Bay, I can see looming storm clouds to the northwest. That's the front. It's almost here.

I am exhausted, but I have gone a total of 150 miles southeast, all under sail. I head for Abraham's Bay, a body of water about five miles long and almost totally surrounded by reefs. There are only two openings, one in the west and one in the east near the settlement. I arrive outside the western cut, and lower my sails. Forget sailing — I want to concentrate on avoiding the heads.

I usually take my GPS coordinates from a chart, if the chart looks good. Here the chart is detailed since this was also a U.S. Navy base in World War II. But I notice in comparing my chart-derived entry point to one in a guidebook that they differ by more than one-half mile. A second guidebook describes a problem in getting GPS coordinates that align with those of the chart. My nervousness increases, and I decide to go with the first guidebook.

I drive in looking carefully for heads. I see breaking water all around me, but do not pass close to a head. The bay is very large. I go toward the beach to get protection from the winds I expect soon to come from the north.

I put out one anchor and dive to check on it. The bottom is sand and grass dotted with tiny oases of corals and sponges. The anchor is set well. As I swim back to the boat the rains come. Once on board I grab my shampoo and have a rainwater shower. I usually skip the soap and use shampoo for both shampoo and soap. I am not quite alone, but the nearer of two boats I can see is about a mile away. I feel no concern about stripping bare for my wash-up.

The rain lasts about ten minutes, and is relatively light. When it ends we have a northwest breeze.

I dry off, dress, and begin to lower the dinghy. The lock I use to chain the dinghy to the boat is frozen, so I spend 15 minutes pouring anticorrosion fluid in it. I find that my locks frequently keep me locked out, but then I have never had a dinghy or motor stolen, so perhaps the effort required to lock up is worthwhile.

Soon I am off at full speed for the shore. Using my tiller extension to steer, I sit on the bow of my dinghy. Our 8-horsepower Nissan outboard really moves the dinghy when I am in it alone. Suddenly I pass over a large patch of excrement-brown sea. Coral! I have a deep sense of panic, but we slip over it without hitting. Excrement-brown can ruin a day, I think, my own unrhymed verse for the sailor's warning poem, *If it's blue, sail right through; if it's white, you just might; if it's green, go through clean; if it's brown, run aground.* Now I go slower, and I watch carefully. Coral is everywhere as I approach land, and it appears to start a little farther out than I remember from the chart.

The beach looks like those at the Marquesas Keys back home, narrow, cluttered, and steep. But the sand is not as hard-packed as the beaches there; this is not a good running beach. Since I am a bit tired I will skip the run. I walk the beach. One end is full of flotsam covering broken coral. Close to shore I

...narrow, cluttered, and steep.

see a foot-long fish swimming in a tight circle, perhaps in pursuit of prey or maybe just busy stirring up the sand for the purpose of finding something to eat. As I look off the beach, I see a circle of breaking seas about a mile or so away. It feels strange and dangerous to be surrounded by reef.

Next morning at 5:30 the weather report from the Coast Guard on radio station NMN is not encouraging. North to northwest winds at 20 to 30 knots, and 9- to 12-foot seas. If my wife was with me I certainly wouldn't leave under these rough conditions. But the wind will be off my aft quarter, and the stress on the boat will not be great. Being an optimist, I assume, of course, that the wind won't rise to much over 20 knots.

The difference between 30-knot winds and 20-knot winds is significant. The stress on the boat grows with the energy transferred from the wind into the kinetic energy of the boat. A 30-knot wind will have more than double the impact of a 20-knot wind (a ratio of 9 to 4). But with the wind from the aft quarter, I do not expect to see more than a 25-knot apparent wind even with 30-knot weather. And with an aft-quarter wind, even if it goes to 30 knots, the boat will not pound into the waves.

I motor out through the hole in the reef, retracing yesterday's route. The wind and seas here in Abraham's Bay are not bad but I see waves breaking over reef on both sides of me, and the brown outlines of coral. I see a big patch of coral ahead to starboard and turn left, a little south of the route I took yesterday. I think the chart is correct. By following the guidebook's coordinates I came in a bit too close to the reef yesterday.

Once out of the bay, I put up the mainsail and head out southeast. If it is only 20 knots I will not need a reef in the main. But soon the seas build and the wind grows to 25 knots. I should have reefed earlier, when it was easy. I decide to try reefing the way the designer of my slab reef system intended.

A word about reefing my main: I try this procedure periodically. It invariably ends with a statement of heartfelt contempt for this single-line reefing system and its designer. The goal of the system is good, to allow the main to be reefed or shortened by a pulling on a single line, using the winch at the mast. But the line travels a long and intricate path through multiple blocks and tight turns. Along most of its length it cannot be seen or adjusted. Should the line bind inside the boom, and *it almost always does bind*, nothing can be done except to release tension and start again. When I first tried this system during a 35-knot blow in Pamlico Sound off the North Carolina coast, I struggled unsuccessfully with it for almost an hour.

My efforts this time are classic in the annals of my attempts at using the reefing system as intended. I work at it for about a half-hour, then settle for an only halfway adequate result. This will do. But if I had tied off the grommets with separate lines at the beginning of my sail it would have taken ten minutes, worked just as well, and looked better.

As the day progresses the waves and seas build. Early on I think that maybe I will see no more than 25 knots today. More than 25 knots and I will regret putting up only one reef. By afternoon the wind is 30 knots and there is foam and spray from big waves. Surely these waves are over 12 feet. Otto is having a tough time. Every gust of wind wheels the boat around, abeam of the seas. Otto corrects and we swing back 30 degrees.

The boat has a strong weather helm (it moves into the wind if uncorrected by rudder) since I shortened the jib. But I shortened the jib to stop the jib from pulling the starboard bow into the sea on each gust. I could fix the balance by putting in a second reef, but under these conditions, I think I'll just put up with it and stay safely in the cockpit.

Good news! After listening to the NMN offshore broadcast at 6 o'clock, I conclude that conditions must be getting better. This assumes, of course, that I fit into the category of "elsewhere" as described in the report. North to northeast winds of 15 to 20 knots and 6- to 9-foot seas are predicted.

I go outside and see my wind gauge measuring 30 knots of wind. The sea is more than a little ruffled, with waves at least 15 feet tall. I admonish the waves, drink in hand, with a clear sense of the righteousness of my complaint. Don't they listen to the forecast?

You may be surprised that I enjoy a drink on these long passages, still underway. In my defense (should I need a defense), let me note that the captain's mood is most important. If not in good spirits, the captain may see less meaning in the trip, and may retreat to the cabin to read.

It is also very unlikely I will run into you out here. Besides, I drink moderately, only a fixed amount, and never, ever dangle over the back rail in big seas with my last drink in hand.

It grows dark. A freighter passes in the far distance, oblivious to these waves that crash and boom around my much smaller craft. I can see some stars. It is a strangely beautiful night, though filled with waves and spray.

I expected to be seasick by now, with all this boat motion, but I'm not. I wonder if my body is accommodating to these rough and rolly seas.

We continue to lurch forward on the gusts, falling back on 20-knot lulls. Our speed ranges from 4 to 10 knots. I note one spurt of 12 knots, too fast for this boat. Occasionally a big wave catches us and crashes over the port side. I have all hatches closed, but the boat is once again developing a coating of salt. There is little bridgedeck pounding, the bane of catamaran sailors. Pounding occurs when a wave hits up from below between the hulls as they did as I crossed the Gulf Stream. With a lot of bridgedeck pounding the catamaran can come to a total standstill in heavy seas because of the drag. But with the wind aft of beam, pounding rarely occurs.

Heading toward North Caicos en route to Big Sand Cay I begin to think of all the things that could go wrong tonight. Soon I will be heading south through Turks Passage. Suppose Otto freaks out in the assault of a following sea? As I turn, I expect the wind to be directly from behind, greatly increasing the likelihood that the boat will have accidental jibes, where the wind or boat shifts so that the wind catches the back side of the sail. I always have a preventer on the boom (a line that keeps the boom from swinging across the boat). But when the main gets backwinded, the stern is pulled across the sea, putting great pressure on the rudders and autopilot, despite the preventer. If Otto goes out, I will have to disassemble it rapidly, not easy in this bouncing boat. We could broach (turn beam to wind and waves) while I struggle for control.

I practice in my mind the process of gaining control. I can to some degree overpower the autopilot actuator, but it is not easy. I will be as fast as I can about disengaging Otto.

What if my GPS goes? I have lost convergence several times this trip. While I have a backup GPS, a Garmin 45, it is not as good as my Garmin 75, and besides the real danger here is loss of satellite signal. My electronics are only three years old. I have just checked the steering. The sails seem fine. At the end of this session of worrying and planning, I conclude that I am all right. Nothing can happen that I can't handle.

I see North Caicos, and I lose my GPS signal. I don't worry. I expect to regain it soon. The lights of North Caicos are regularly spaced and seem to go on forever. This is a big island.

My GPS is still not functioning. So it's back to basics: I will use my compass. I turn on my compass light, but the bulb must be burned out. Well, OK, I'll light the compass with my flashlight. Surely I can make this leg of the journey without GPS. The currents are tough to estimate here, but I have the lights at Drum Point, and on Grand Turk, as guides. — Ah, GPS is back. Forget the lights, forget the compass. GPS is on the job!

The BBC keeps me amused with a Paul Robeson documentary. What an incredible man! He spoke twenty-five languages, and sang folk songs in so many, including Chinese. Paul Robeson singing Mandarin Chinese. It actually sounds like Chinese to me. And then folk songs in Russian. These are tough languages. I studied both of them, without much success.

About midnight I see a sailboat approaching. It appears to be on a collision course with me, and closing fast. This boat is sailing well-reefed, and it is large, with two masts. At first I can't believe it is really coming right at me. After all, this is a big ocean, and this two-masted ship is only the second boat I have seen on this trip! It seems improbable. I have my radio off, unfortunately. I need to develop new habits. Just about the time I begin to think of wandering down to the navigation station on the starboard side to turn on the juice to my radio, I realize we could actually collide. We are coming far too close in these rough seas! I decide to turn 30 degrees into the wind, taking the wind on the beam for a bit. At almost the same time, the other boat turns 30 degrees off the wind. If he turned the other way he would have come to a stop. We avoid collision, but not by much. Good thing I made no attempt to sleep tonight. I turn the radio on. I wonder if he tried to contact me. I decide not to call him. No point inviting a rebuke.

About 3 o'clock in the morning the seas seem to have died back a bit. I sit awhile on the hardtop, watching the waves. It is relaxing. I see that a big north swell is developing, augmenting the seas. This is no doubt the result of the gale that has been raging several hundred miles to my north.

Drenched again! Out of nowhere a big wave hits us on the beam, sending buckets of water over me, and splashing the sail up to the second reef point. All the instruments and my seat down below are soaked. Back at George

Town some cruisers were telling me I needed to put up my dodger (a snap-on canvas-and-clear-plastic windshield) to keep me and the instruments dry in rough seas. My response was that I liked feeling the breeze, and didn't like the loss in visibility. The dodger would not have kept me dry from this wave, I am thinking. I was hit slightly aft of the beam. Big waves have been breaking around me all day and night. This must have been a big one that broke in the wrong place. I go in to change my clothes.

Around 4 o'clock I pick up a passenger, an exhausted bird. I cannot see it well in the dark. It sits on the lifeline, balancing precariously. At one point it loses its balance, flies off, and shows up on the port bow pulpit, a slightly better choice of perch. As I turn into Turks passage and adjust the main, the bird retreats to the dinghy. At daybreak it busies itself with some preening, fluffs his feathers as if to say, *Well, I handled that successfully, didn't I?*, and flies away. I have precisely the same thought as I sail into morning.

...an exhausted bird.

About 10 o'clock Monday morning , April 13, I arrive off Big Sand Cay. I put down one anchor in very bouncy 20-foot water, in a very sandy area. This is a very rolly anchorage, with no protection from the north wind. Perhaps I am so tired it will not bother me.

I dive on the anchor. It lies deep in the sand. I see nothing on the bottom but sand. One 4-foot barracuda pauses, looks me in the eye, and continues on.

The water contains thousands of jellyfish, about a half-inch in diameter. They look like tiny pulsating barrels. I grab my underwater camera, hoping to capture them on film, but they are elusive. I take pictures of the sandy bottom instead, and the bottom of *Top Cat* behind a raft of sargassum weed.

... the bottom of Top Cat behind a raft of sargassum weed.

Big Sand Cay is an uninhabited island, part of the Turks and Caicos Islands, a British Crown Colony. Though it is forbidden, since I have not cleared British customs or immigration, I dinghy briefly to the island. I land in rough surf, and pull the dinghy up high on a steep beach. I will stay only a couple of minutes because I fear a wave will take the dinghy.

I land in rough surf, and pull the dinghy up high...

The sand is very soft, totally unsuitable for running. People have been here; there is a lean-to. On the other side of the island I see a reef, and lots of flotsam and jetsam. I look for a bottle for my son's collection, but none of them are particularly interesting. The cliffs on the west side of the island are really pretty. It is amazing how much life clings to these rugged rocks.

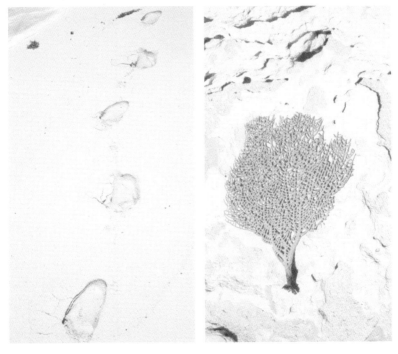

...unsuitable for running.   *...lots of flotsam and jetsam.*

About 4 o'clock in the afternoon three sailboats arrive, and all anchor close to me. We converse on the radio. They have come from Ambergris, south of South Caicos, and will leave for the Dominican Republic tomorrow.

Van Sant, in his *Gentleman's Guide to Passages South*, recommends a route through the Turks and Caicos, with a last stop at on the Caicos bank at Ambergris, then across the Turks Passage to Big Sand Cay. For cruisers going south, Van Sant's book is the route guide, and the cruisers I have talked to adhere to his routes religiously. I have read his book carefully, and found it excellent. But I didn't really want to go through the Caicos bank, full of coral hazards, if I could find a way around it under favorable weather. The cruisers discuss their rough crossing of Turks Passage. I leave the radio on, and listen to them chatter for a while.

It is amazing how much life clings to these rugged rocks.

Morning comes, all too soon. I listen to the offshore weather report on NMN at 5:30. It is an effort to get up this early after skipping sleep night before last, but I am eager to go on and want to hear the forecast. The prediction is for northeast to east winds of 15 to 20 knots with 6- to 8-foot seas. This seems adequate to me for crossing to Luperon in the Dominican Republic today. I plan to leave late in the afternoon. One of my three fellow cruisers leaves at about 3:30 for Luperon. The second and third decide to wait for Herb Hilgenberg's weather interpretation at 5 o'clock. Herb is an amateur weather forecaster and cruiser who interprets offshore weather each day on SSB. I decide to leave at 4:30, satisfied with the NMN report this morning.

In the afternoon, I begin the process of getting underway. I start the autopilot, then reassemble it. (I could damage the belt if I start it while assembled and engaged.) Then I start both engines and put them both in gear. This reduces some of the pressure from the wind on the anchor rode. Still, with 15 to 20 knots of wind the anchor is difficult to bring in. I find that there are three activities on the boat that take just about all the strength I have. The hardest task is pulling the anchor in against a brisk wind. Others are rapidly furling the jib under 15 or more knots of wind and taking the 55-pound Nissan engine on and off the dinghy. I take the motor off the dinghy and secure it on

Top Cat before each passage, putting it back on the dinghy when I reach each destination. My procedure is relatively high risk, and requires that I support the motor more or less in one hand balanced precariously on the back step. I could do this using my small lift, but it would take much longer and I would risk smashing it into the solar panel that bridges the davits at the stern.

Today I struggle mightily with the anchor. I use gloves, and pull the line in with the help of the engines. It is difficult since there is nobody to steer the boat, and it is frequently off track. I pull the boat around with the anchor rode. Then finally I use brute force to break the anchor free of its sand entombment. Once the anchor is up I work hard to get the main up with a single reef, then get the boat moving out and around South Rocks. Finally I am on my way, but already feeling exhausted. Lifting the anchor has worn me out.

I call back once I have cleared the Cay and surrounding rocks to tell the remaining cruisers the conditions at sea. It is rough, with over 20 knots of wind. The cruisers say that Herb advised them to stay. They nevertheless decide to leave, departing about an hour behind me. Both are ketches, sailboats with two masts. They are larger, and probably faster than me.

Winds remain high and seas large hours after we are in deep water. I am in constant contact with the others by radio. We have hope that as we approach the big island of Hispaniola with its 3000-foot mountains the land will have a mitigating effect on the wind and seas, as described in Van Sant's book.

Even though I am on a beam reach or broad reach for the passage, the boat is soon soaked with spray. I sail with a reefed main and a mostly furled jib. Each time I step out of the cabin to check the instruments and sails I am doused with spray. The boat balance is not good. I let out the main, further spoiling the efficiency of the sail by assuring that the main is backwinded by the jib. My goal is to moderate my speed of over 7 knots so as to reduce the tendency of the boat to drive into the waves. I also regulate the speed so that I can arrive shortly after sunrise in Luperon, not in the dark. I don't want to arrive much after sunrise, either, since conditions get worse at sea as the day progresses. It is important to arrive at the end of any passage during daylight so I find that I adjust the sails to slow the boat almost as often as I adjust to more efficiently use the wind.

I enjoy the sunset with my drink, then heat up stew for dinner. I enjoy standing or sitting (when conditions permit) on the leeward back steps, watching the rush of water go by. Here there is little spray. I hold onto the rails firmly, since I do not consider it rough enough to have my harness and jack line. I trust my good balance and strong grip. I am fortunate that my wife is not here to see me taking such chances!

Later I listen to an audio book on Eastern philosophy, and try to remain awake for the passage. Fifteen miles from land I see what looks like a floating island. Shortly afterward I hear the cruiser in front of me raise the island on the radio. The island is not an island after all, but a tug pulling a large barge. A long towline connects the two. Sleeping sailors aboard boats that pass between this pair would be rather unpleasantly aroused from their dreams.

At ten miles from land, I still see no overall moderation in wind or seas. The winds continue to be somewhat gusty, with lulls of 15-knot winds, and highs well over 20 knots. The sea is very lumpy, but not as rough as the seas I saw on the passage from Mayaguana.

I reach Hispaniola ahead of the lead cruiser, a little after sunrise. I am met by two people in a skiff from Puerto Blanco Marina. They talked to us earlier. They have come to pilot us past the reefs on both sides of the cut into Luperon. Apparently several boats have gone aground on the reef in recent months since the loss of the red sea buoy marking the entrance. Big waves are breaking over a reef on the east side of the entrance; these are the breakers the arriving cruiser first sees. Cruisers may then mistakenly move too far west in their efforts to miss the east reef. The marina was now trying to assist all first-time arriving cruisers into the harbor. I am thankful for the assist; I quickly douse my sails and power up the engines. I follow them, using the autopilot. Otto goes bananas now and then in these rough seas, but he handles the job.

Soon I am in out of the rough seas and into Luperon's very protected harbor. I disassemble Otto, and pilot myself the rest of the way. The harbor is mentioned as an excellent refuge in a hurricane, and it is easy to see why. There is protection from the wind on all sides, with a sand and mud bottom. The edges appear to be lined with mangroves. The water is quiet, a welcome relief.

I quickly put down one anchor at the end of the west harbor, in front of about twenty other sailboats, and one powerboat. The other cruisers appear to be a little bigger than my boat; there is another catamaran here. This is quiet, muddy water of a quality that suggest that one does not dive on an anchor here or use this water to wash dishes.

The harbor is full of the smells of the countryside, smells absent from the Bahamas. The hills around me are full of cows and chickens. I can see many planted fields. Some look like sugarcane.

The water is quiet, a welcome relief.

Over the next three hours the three sailboats that came in with me from Big Sand Cay are led in one by one.

One anchors nearby, then later moves to a position behind me. A second first tries to anchor at this end, then the other end. The third spends some time traveling around the harbor with his anchor in the water, looking for the perfect spot.

I am not nearly so fussy.

I wait for customs and immigration. After an hour or so, a shabby wooden boat with a small outboard motor arrives with three local men. One, the driver, stays on the small boat. The other, dressed in street clothes with a revolver stuck in under his belt on the back, climbs aboard. His English is not good, but my Spanish is worse. He is from immigration. He comes with an interpreter whom he beckons to join us. With help from the third man, we fill out his form, and I pay a $10 fee.

 In another two hours the same boat and driver arrive, but this time with two new people. One, I am told, is a dock boy, who asks if I need any gas. He is the interpreter on this trip. I give him two 6-gallon containers to fill. The other says he is the customs official, from the office of the *Commandante*. I seem to satisfy his needs rapidly. I give the men a couple of cans of diet Coke. I am not charged for this transaction.

Between visits from these officials I am visited by a French cruiser from a 42-foot Catana catamaran. He asks about the sea conditions, and seems tired of waiting for good weather to make his departure. He sees no prospects of leaving soon. He is on his way to St. Thomas and St. Martin, but recently spent four months in Miami. Before that he was in Belize and in Mexico.

The pair from the local marina that led me in came by to invite me to a briefing on Luperon they are giving tonight at the marina bar. Unfortunately, I fall asleep and don't arrive at the marina until after they have left.

I have dinner with four cruising couples. The dinner is good, but the service is exceptionally slow. We talk mainly about cruising, weather, and routes. Several mention that they took about a month to get here from George Town following the Van Sant route. It took me only five very tough days. I ask about crossing the Mona Passage. One suggests waiting for a front. Nobody likes Van Sant's suggestion of two nights and one day for the crossing.

Luperon's greatest attraction is the harbor. It is small and the perfect depth for the cruiser. No other harbor in the Dominican Republic is nearly as well protected from weather. It is so well protected that my boat barely moves despite 20-knot easterly winds over the open water. Decades ago the Dominican Republic designated Luperon as an entry port for cruisers, and so the cruisers come! The city is poor, and small. I am not sure it is helped much by cruisers, who are very often not big spenders. It appears strange to have so much wealth afloat in this small harbor and so little of it on land.

The Dominicans are friendly, and do not appear resentful that their visitors have more money invested in their dinghies than they earn in a year. I walk the streets of the city, and out into the countryside, smiling and waving at the locals. *"Ola! Ola!"* I call to the people I pass. Motorcycles, cars, and bikes are available for renting, but I like the exercise. Besides, motoring looks danger-ous. All along the road just outside the city are little crosses surrounded by pots of dying flowers. The motorbikes whiz by at alarming speeds. I don't see a speed limit sign.

I walk the streets of the city...

...and out into the countryside...

There are many small pickup trucks and cars loaded with amplifiers and enormous speakers going up and down the streets booming out their messages. I see no sign of TV or radio here. Instead, the word is spread by amplified sound. There is evidence that a political campaign is going on. I see banners and signs, and take a picture of a party headquarters plastered with pictures of candidates.

...a party headquarters plastered with pictures of candidates.

The other cruisers sign up for a series of tours. They all crowd into minivans, and head out to Puerto Plata, to the waterfalls, or to Santo Domingo. These people are convinced they will be waiting awhile for better weather. The man in the house closest to the dinghy dock asks me if he can give me a tour of the falls. I decline for a second time; also for the second time he points out that he lives in the first house, and I can easily find him if I change my mind. His house measures about 10 feet on a side, and is obviously without indoor plumbing. Apparently constructed from discarded lumber, it has a thatch roof. This is one of the sorriest-looking houses in town. I wonder uncharitably if the house is part of his sales pitch. Perhaps he figures that if you don't want to go on the tour, once you see his house, you will take pity on him and hire him anyway or maybe just give him some money. The cruisers later report that the falls tour is very nice. It is possible to slide from one to another of the falls that cascade down the mountain.

Dominoes appears to be a popular pasttime here...

I watch the Dominicans on the street going about their daily activities. Dominoes appears to be a popular pastime here, attracting plenty of kibitzers. I buy a few small items from the gift shops and the market, a small grocery store offering a variety of items. Those that are locally produced, like the rum and ham that I purchase, are reasonably priced. I find the local *Presidente* beer very good. Imported items are expensive. I decline to fill my propane tank since it requires a *motorconcho* (a motorbike with passenger seat for hire). I still have about ten days' supply of propane left.

I take a walk along a forest path to the ocean. I see many tropical birds, but they are all too quick and I cannot take their pictures. I nearly step on one bird's nest (perhaps a pheasant). The ensuing flurry and squawk almost gives me a heart attack. Later on my walk, I get close enough to some butterflies to take pictures of them.

I get close enough to some butterflies to take pictures of them.

When I reach the ocean, the water looks much calmer than when I arrived. I watch waves wash up through holes in the craggy limestone lining the shore. They explode noisily into geysers.

I watch waves wash up through holes in the rock...

Perfect Paul on station NMN predicts today, Friday, April 17, that the wind will slow to 15 knots tomorrow night. Sounds good to me. I will depart.

Only one boat has left since I arrived, and it headed west to Florida. I may be the first out going east. All the cruisers I have talked to rely almost exclusively on Herb Hilgenberg for weather advice. Herb goes from one boater on his net to the next, communicating with cruisers all around the North Atlantic. First the boater supplies his or her conditions. Then Herb gives him a weather forecast for his specific location. Herb is fairly cautious, I gather. The advantage to the cruiser is that the forecast is tailored, and he doesn't have to think for himself or even pay attention to the radio forecasts. With NMN one must concentrate hard during Perfect Paul's content-rich report. I can listen to Herb, but since I do not have a transmitter I cannot ask him for the tailored advice that the others do.

I must inform the *Commandante* that I will be leaving. I know precisely where he is because his building has a large antenna. But I can't figure out how to get there. I can see no route over the land. How can this be? Fortunately I see the immigration man with his interpreter on a motorcycle. I flag them down, and the interpreter offers to take me to the *Commandante's* office for a tip. The path to the *Commandante's* office is behind some shacks. Then we cross a small mangrove creek. Once a bridge crossed this creek, the interpreter explains, but it fell apart a couple of months ago. So we cross the muddy creek by boat, pulling ourselves across using a line connecting the boat to each side of the creek. Climbing in and out of the boat is not easy. I am glad that I asked for help getting here. On my own I probably never would have discovered this route to the most important office in town.

The interpreter talks to one of the *Commandante's* assistants who doesn't speak English. He fills out a *Despacho de Buques* for my release. With paper in hand I start to leave when the assistant emerges again to inform the interpreter who tells me that the *Commandante* requests another $10. What for, I ask? I visit the *Commandante* in person to see about the fee. He sits in a small room devoid of furniture except for a wooden chair, wooden desk, and telephone. He is in his 30s, I guess, and without a uniform. He does not speak English, communicating with me through the interpreter. He says that immigration and customs are two different groups, and he, too, must have $10. While I am pretty sure this is not true I think these people need the money more than I do. I give him the $10. I also give his assistant a five-peso note as a tip, which he had requested through the interpreter. I have just about spent all my money now. I could go to a bank in Puerto Plata to get more money, but I am not sure now that I have enough for the *motorconcho* ride. Besides, I want to leave. I will pick up money in Puerto Rico.

I decide to go at dusk. It doesn't take long sitting in Luperon harbor to sense the cycle of the winds. It is quiet in the morning, picking up around 11. It remains strong from noon to 1 o'clock, then begin to drop a little. By late afternoon the winds are much reduced. Without a front, I decide evening is the time to set sail.

...we cross the muddy creek by boat, pulling ourselves across using a line connecting the boat to each side of the creek.

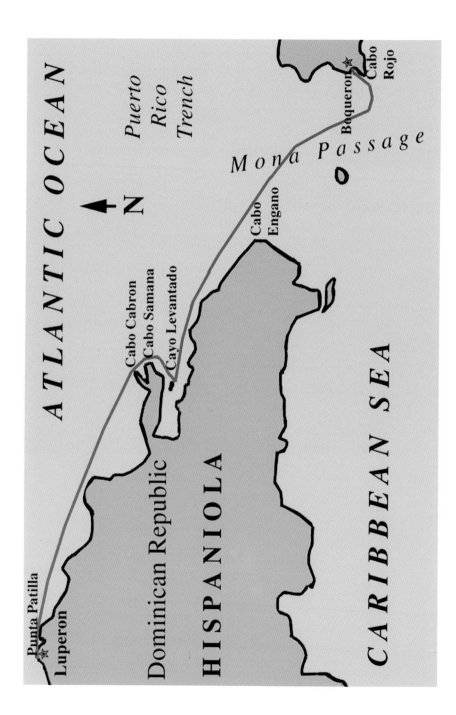

5: Sailing in the Lee of Hispaniola
and Crossing the Mona Passage

At 6:30, with about an hour of light left, I begin the process of leaving. I pull up my anchor slowly, cleaning the rode and chain with my rode brush as I pull it aboard. The task takes me 15 minutes, but is not hard to do in these protected waters. While motoring out toward the harbor entrance I prepare the mainsail with a single reef, then pause briefly to pull it up. Then I turn north and head to sea.

Once clear of the reefs I reassemble Otto, traveling east into about 10 knots of wind. The wind is definitely lighter than I expected, but the sea is still very bouncy. With the wind out of the northeast I am able to get some assist from the main, but not enough to shut down both engines. I kill one, and pull it up out of the water, reducing drag. Using only one engine gives me a little better gas mileage and reduces by half the total number of engine hours, the factor that drives my maintenance schedule.

After a couple of hours I am past Punta Patilla, and am able to travel southeast. This allows me to pick up more wind. I reduce the engine speed, still traveling well at about 5 knots. The seas seem to be calming a bit, but I decide that 5 knots is good enough for me.

I keep a changing set of optional waypoints — should the weather get worse I will head for shelter. As the evening wears on, the weather holds steady. I listen to BBC, and Radio Netherlands. I see no other boats.

In the morning the winds pick up a bit, but not past 15 knots. I press on, creating a new set of optional stopping points. I still have one engine on, but only at about half speed. I get occasional spray. It is not windy, but the seas are rough. There is also a swell from the gales still raging to the north.

My GPS begins to ring for no apparent reason. I clean it off, push some buttons. I talk encouragingly to it, but it cannot be soothed and continues to ring. Perhaps it has had one too many dousings with seawater. Next time I will bring the dodger. Eventually the ringing stops. The dousings have not affected its function; it still works fine. With no companionship I find myself talking to Otto and Geeps (the GPS might as well have a name, too, I think, and so I have christened it Geeps) quite a bit. Sometimes I even talk to myself. I am not sure long solo voyages are my cup of tea.

I sail all day, watching the coast and sea. Dolphins come by to play off my bow for a while. I see many flying fish. And I watch the coast. The mountains and meadows remind me a bit of our American West. Hispaniola is mountainous, but with palm trees lining the ridges.

Hispaniola is mountainous, with palm trees lining the ridges.

As evening approaches the wind and sea continues to hold; I decide to skip the harbor at Escondido and continue on around Cabo Cabron.

It is very dark by early evening. Moonrise is several hours away. The sky is covered with clouds. I can barely make out the mountains that mark the coast. I move from *cabo* to *cabo* (cape to cape), so I see little of land until I reach the next cape. I see occasional lights on the coast, but generally not on the capes. Each of them looms menacingly out of the darkness as I approach. The wind picks up near each, but not appreciably.

The sky begins to lighten as the moon rises. This allows me to look around a bit, and I am alarmed. The moonlight shows me storm clouds. I can see sheets of rain dropping from one storm cell directly ahead of me. A good soaking wouldn't hurt me, but there are probably winds, too. Perhaps lightning, although I don't see it. I decide to alter course to avoid the storm.

I successfully sail around the storm cell. It seems to dissipate behind me. I can see other very dark storm cells too. As the night wears on I dodge several more.

By morning the storms have passed, and the wind continues to be light. I sail about a half mile off Cabo Cabron, and a mile off Cabo Samana. Still I feel the effects of each cape, with stronger wind and rougher seas. The wind tends to hug the coast as it rounds these mountainous capes, creating stiffer headwinds.

By morning the storms have passed...

My strategy is to tack back and forth a little off the wind with the engine on and the mainsail up. I tack too close to the wind to use the jib around the capes. Tacking saves gas, and greatly reduces the bounce of the boat in 6-foot seas. Even slowed by tacking I determine that I can make harbor off Samana by dusk.

Cabo Cabron and Cabo Samana are empty of people, but are scenic, with rocky cliffs and beautiful tropical trees.

As I turn southwest around Cabo Samana, the wind picks up a bit, and I cut the engine. I get a little more spray. The sea and the wind are definitely increasing as the day progresses, a familiar pattern.

As dusk approaches I am resigned to hearing the 6 o'clock NMN offshore forecast while I am at sea. I don't like to do this because keeping watch distracts from the concentration I need to catch everything Perfect Paul has to say, and also because the antenna wire is connected through the starboard hatch. I keep the wire unattached while at sea since the hatch must normally remain closed to keep the salon dry. I must now reattach the wire.

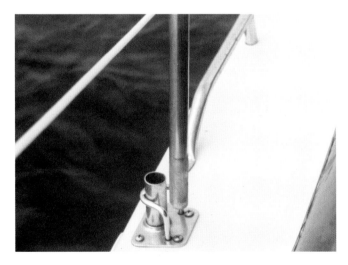

The stanchion is pulled out!

I begin to creep around the starboard side, clutching the lifeline for balance, on my way to the antenna at the front of the boat. Suddenly the lifeline comes loose. The stanchion is pulled out! I am startled, but regain my balance. Should I be wearing my harness, with a line attached to a jack line down the middle of the boat? I would, if it were much rougher. I attach the antenna, and listen to the weather report.

I turn east past Punta Balandra and head in toward the town of Samana. The wind is from behind me here, and the sea undulates with large swells. These conditions are particularly difficult for sailing. The swell causes the boat to swing from 30 or more degrees first to one side then to the other off my direction of sail and then the main is backwinded and slams against the preventer. When this happens Otto loses control. He beeps noisily to get my attention. *I'm losing her, Captain!* When the wind is back on the right side of the sail, usually with my help, the boat handles much better, and Otto does fine.

I see big rocks in the water off the coast ahead, and a sailboat clearly in trouble on the reef to the east of Cayo Leventado. I am very tired. I decide it is time to take down the main, and motor in the remaining few miles. I turn *Top Cat* into the wind and with Otto at the helm, I lower the main. This is not easy, since Otto has a hard time staying pointed into the wind under these conditions. The rocks loom ahead. I move more quickly, and shortly have the main down and Otto repointed downwind. I turn on two engines for good control. It's getting dark and I begin to see rocks everywhere.

Under the setting sun I head for Cayo Leventado. I decide to anchor here rather than go three miles farther west to Samana. I don't want to be bothered with customs again since I plan to leave early tomorrow for Puerto Rico.

Big rocks in the water appear hazardous as I come in on this very dark night. Two buoys mark the channel. They appear to be real buoys, and they are not lighted. One, clearly marked on my chart as lighted, appears dead ahead of me. Fortunately, I have been using it as a waypoint, and have been looking out for it. Still, I could have easily have hit it in the darkness. I first saw it when we were about two boatlengths away, and passed within thirty feet of it. (In the morning I see how substantial it is and I am glad I did not hit it.)

...I am glad I did not hit it.

I approach my anchorage waypoint and am alarmed once again. I see lights on Cayo Leventado and waves breaking over a white sandy beach less than 100 feet ahead, yet I am in over 100 feet of water! The sea bottom in this area clearly mirrors the land. Up and down, up and down. The water is 120 feet deep next to rocks looming up out of the water. There are patches of shallows here and there. Watching the depth meter while driving in is interesting, educational, and alarming, though not necessarily in that order.

...I marvel at how pretty Cayo Levantado is.

When finally I reach 20-foot water, I feel like I can reach out and touch the shore. This is untenable. I will not anchor so close to the land. I reach for the chart and select a second anchorage, one farther off the west end of the island. I punch in a new waypoint for Geeps and point Otto toward it. We finally reach water that seems shallow enough, and still clear of the island. Down goes the anchor. No anchor diving tonight. It is pitch dark, and I am exhausted. I set the anchor carefully, backing down with my engines to tuck it in well.

I sleep like the dead for 10 hours. In the morning I marvel at how pretty Cayo Leventado is. It is clearly a park or a resort with an excellent beach. There are small boats to rent, but I see few people here on this weekday morning.

I quickly fix the stanchion that pulled out during my passage. I brought extra rivets and a rivet gun for just such an eventuality. It takes only a few minutes to put in two new rivets to reattach the stanchion to its base. I make a quick inspection of the other stanchions around the deck. They are firmly seated.

...he crosses the oar handle ends while rowing.

I pull up the anchor and head out. I missed the weather report this morning, but last night's Perfect Paul sounded promising. We are on the edge of two weather-reporting areas, the southwest North Atlantic and the Eastern Caribbean. On the other side of the Mona Passage we will cross to the Eastern Caribbean. I get two conflicting forecasts here, and decide to split the difference. I conclude we should have 15 knots of wind, from a direction somewhere between northeast and southeast.

There are working fishermen here. I see them in their rowboats, attending their traps. The floats on their traps are plastic gallon bottles. I'd better not hit one. These men must be strong with all the rowing required to tend traps. I watch one man carefully; he crosses the oar handle ends while rowing.

As I pass the east end of Cayo Leventado I search for the sailboat I saw floundering last night. There is no trace of the boat. Instead I see locals in a small sailboat.

...I see locals in a small sailboat.

With one engine on and the main up, I head out from Punta Balandra on a direct course to the northeast tip of the deep shoals reaching eastward from Cabo Engaño. The shoals are hundreds of feet deep, but are marked as hazardous on my chart, with rip currents and turbulent seas. From the edge of the shoal I will turn a little more southeast on a path to Cabo Rojo at the southwest corner of Puerto Rico. The distance is about the same as the run from Luperon to Samana, over 120 nautical miles. If the weather holds I should be there tomorrow afternoon.

A good part of this trip is over the deep bank on the east end of the Dominican Republic. The water ranges from twenty feet to hundreds of feet before dropping off to ocean depths. After that we cross through the deep water of the Mona Passage to Puerto Rico. To the north of us is the Puerto Rico Trench, the second deepest ocean trench in the world.

I am astounded to find that once again I am on a collision course with another vessel. This time it is a small fishing boat, perhaps 15 feet long, with an outboard engine. He appears to be anchored, but he is in 300 feet of water. Perhaps he has a drogue. His little boat is bouncing so much that I see him, then I don't. I change course by 20 degrees. Without that correction I would have been on top of him. Instead, I pass him 60 feet away. We wave to each other. His job is a tough one, 20 miles from shore and bobbing like a cork.

Evening arrives. The sunset is great. I have my drink, then dinner, then I listen to an audio book. The night is dark, good for stargazing. The wind remains light, about 10 knots, and from the southeast. I continue to motor with some assist from the main. The moon rises about 2 o'clock, ruining my stargazing. With the additional light I can now see the waves. They look moderate, without whitecaps. I am bouncing, but I am not uncomfortable. I really enjoy this late-night sail. It is peaceful, and would be much more so without the engine.

As the sun rises, I look for breakfast. The wind and seas continue to be moderate. I am feeling good. I make small adjustments in my engine speed to arrive well before dark at Cabo Rojo. Early in the morning I get a call on VHF from a passing sailboat. He is several miles away, he says, off my starboard beam. I search, and there he is, barely visible. We talk for 20 minutes. He is heading for Florida. He tells me that the place to be in Puerto Rico is Salinas. All the cruisers are there. There were about 50 boats there when he left.

About 30 miles from land I take the opportunity to empty my holding tank. With just me aboard, the tank fills in about three weeks. I wonder what the stay-in-port cruisers do? I don't want to think too long about this.

All good things must come to an end. Around noon the wind begins to pick up, as it usually does at this time of day. I start to get spray, and my forward progress really slows. I am forced to tack to keep my speed up and reduce the spray. Instead of a 2 o'clock arrival I start to hope for 4.

At 3 o'clock the wind is much stronger, at least 20 knots, and directly from Cabo Rojo, my destination. I begin to think of alternatives.

By 4 I am seeing storm clouds, and have 26 knots of apparent wind. I am going about 3 knots, and I am well off my bearing to anchorage. I decide to give it up, and head off the wind to Boqueron. If I am to get hit by a storm, that would be the better anchorage. Further, I now doubt that I can make Cabo Rojo in the light given my current progress.

Off the wind I have no trouble reaching Boqueron's harbor. The entrance reef is clearly marked by with a buoy. I have arrived in Puerto Rico, USCG territory. I sail in and join about 20 other yachts anchored off the Boqueron beach. I check in with customs on my cellular phone. It works! They ask me to call again when I reach Ponce, presumably to be inspected. I am exhausted. I sleep well.

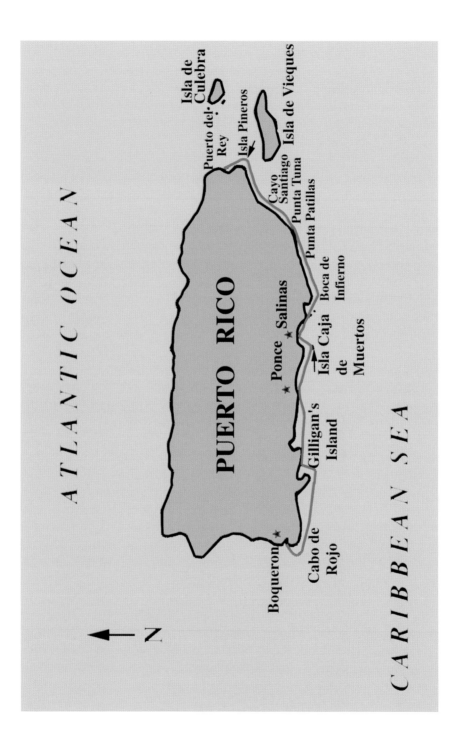

6: Sailing Puerto Rico's Southern Coast

Boqueron is a small town with a good harbor for the cruiser: a sand bottom and plenty of room. The beach here is beautiful, but it is not a good running beach. I like isolated beaches, beaches without people. Private, and quiet. I will skip the run again today.

Instead, I take a walk in town. I visit the U.S. Post Office, and mail a few letters. I pass the fire station and two schools. I see many local people. They are not as friendly as the people in the Dominican Republic. I visit the ATM machine, which recognizes my bankcard and supplies me with money and my current bank balance. My ATM transaction makes me think about home.

The roads look like U.S. roads...

The roads look like U.S. roads and the infrastructure reminds me of home, but all the signs are in Spanish. The schoolchildren wear uniforms. Those I pass chatter to each other in Spanish, though I know from reading the titles of their textbooks that they study English. I stop at the supermarket and buy a few things. Everything is labeled in Spanish. I buy tomatoes and lettuce, the only two vegetables available, and sandwich meat and bread. I can find no English-language newspapers.

This is clearly not the United States. I marvel at the fact that after a century of U.S. rule, this island remains thoroughly Spanish. In French-ruled islands, the people speak French. In English-ruled islands, the people speak English. But here, the people speak Spanish. Back at the boat I check out the AM radio. All the strong stations, about fifteen of them, are in Spanish. I find one weak station from the U.S. Virgin Islands (USVI) in English.

I change the oil in my port engine. I have been using the port engine for the last couple of hundred miles, and the oil is black. Now I will have to find a place that will take the old oil. I will try the marina in St. Thomas, USVI. I also try to clean out some of the salt deposits in the engine, and loosen up the linkages with WD-40. The idle has not been right, and the controls are sticking. After the oil change and clean up, the engine sounds much better.

I am finally beginning to feel warm. I am at 17 degrees latitude and no longer need a long-sleeved shirt, even in the wind.

My neighbors in the harbor are a French family in a large French catamaran, a couple with two adolescent children. They leave for the Dominican Republic before noon. I decide to sail over to Cabo Rojo in the late afternoon so I can go east early in the morning, if the weather looks good. Buoys mark the reef for me. This is easy!

The wind and seas are fine; I spend my time watching the local fisherman. For reasons that escape me, one comes up past me on my starboard side and crosses over to my port beam. He throws out two lines, one on each side of his boat, and slows down. He has no fishing poles, just lines on reels. I wonder if I will run into him. In less than 30 seconds he pulls in a fish! Perhaps he can see the school through the water — perhaps he knows that my boat attracts fish. Who knows why he has chosen to fish here, or why he has had such quick success?

...I spend my time watching the local fisherman.

I see a radar blimp that looks just like Fat Albert over Cudjoe Key back home. Fat Albert, tethered to the ground, carries a radar high into the sky to look for small planes smuggling drugs into the Keys. I suppose the blimp here has the same purpose.

I arrive early at Cabo Rojo, but not early enough. There is already a boat here. This place is small, but looks strangely like Long Key Bight. Same bottom, same mangroves, same birds. I anchor close to the other boat.

I take a short dinghy ride around. I like this place. It does remind me of the Keys. Shallow water, mangroves, birds, and all.

I dinghy over to talk to the people on the other boat, two men in their late twenties or early thirties. Yes, we are going the same way. Surprise, surprise: they are following the Van Sant route. I tell them that I am a rebel and do my own thing. I tell them I will reach Ponce in two days, not Van Sant's required three.

In the morning I work at getting out before those young guys, and I succeed. I round the cape around 6 in the morning and head into the Caribbean Sea.

They follow 10 minutes behind me, bucking the wind and seas. We are definitely beating to windward here. The wind is channeled along this coast. Follow the coastline and you have to go into the wind. The seas are likely to be high with a southeast wind such as we have had. This is equivalent in effect to the northeast wind I had off the north coast of Hispaniola. If the wind continues out of the southeast, cruising this coast will be difficult.

I tack out, then in. It is slow going, and I want to stop by noon, before the really strong wind starts blowing. It seems the young guys believe they will be better off at sea. They go far off shore and seem to make no better progress than I do with shorter tacks up the coast. I notice gleefully at about 11 o'clock that we are about parallel, but I am near my destination and they are five miles off shore! Nothing like a bit of competition to stir the soul, especially when I am in the lead!

Another fisherman turns up in front of me. I am beginning to see a pattern. One of these times I will run into somebody.

I am headed for a place the locals call Gilligan's Island, after the island in the TV show by that name. I must enter the protected waters near the island through a cut in the reef. It is rough water, and I have about 15 knots of wind. I see breaking waves to the left and right. The charts for Puerto Rico are reliable U.S. charts, so I must be doing the right thing here, but entering with so much breaking water is unnerving. I make it through, into calmer water. I anchor to the east of a sailboat here ahead of me.

I take a quick dinghy trip around to survey the place. The empty beach, Punta Ballena on the Puerto Rican mainland, looks good for running. I come back for my running shoes, and quickly head out again. I pull my dinghy up on shore. As I begin to put on my running shoes, a small ferryboat full of people pulls up next to me. A man jumps off in two feet of water and hauls the boat up on the sand. Then five people in bathing suits pile out; my isolated running beach is no longer isolated! Since I already have one shoe on, I finish the job and put the other one on. These people are locals, and they have come to stay for awhile. The only way here is by ferry, they say.

I start my run. The beach is about a mile and a half long. At the other end is a road, and another dozen or so people. The beach is covered with flotsam and jetsam, more than I have ever seen in any other place, more per linear foot of beach than on the Atlantic side of Sands Key in Key Biscayne, and that's saying a lot! The beach faces southeast, and apparently is the receptacle for anything thrown into the water to the south. I conclude that it is never cleaned; no eager Girl Scout troop or Earth Day crew with trash bags visits this place. The beach at the west end where I started looks devastated. All the palm trees are dead. The locals say they suspect someone came in and poisoned the trees. The authorities have begun a replanting program.

All the palm trees are dead.

My run is all right, but the sand here is a little too soft and the beach is downright ugly. The locals advise me to go to Gilligan's Island to have a really good time. I return to the boat to drop off my running shoes and pick up my snorkeling gear, then head to Gilligan's Island by dinghy. On the charts this place is called Cayos de Cana Gorda, but all the people I talk to refer to it as Gilligan's Island. On arrival, I leave my dinghy at the dock and head for the office. The man in the office does not speak English and I can find no map of the place. Although I enjoy trying to communicate in my feeble Spanish, this man will not participate. He points. That is all he will do. I find that I can generally figure out what the signs say, but I have a tough time with the spoken word. I wander around the island. Many trails, and also many people. The people

...a ferry going back and forth almost continuously...

are on the beach and in the water on the north side, the side opposite the
Caribbean Sea. Two channels have been cut through the island, and they are
full of people snorkeling. I snorkel a bit, and I talk to the young people I meet,
who speak English well. The channels, through which a weak current of water
flows, are lined with mangroves and filled with small and colorful reef fish.
The young people I talk to don't know much about the other side, so I decide
to dinghy around the island, and snorkel there.

The other side is protected by a reef several hundred feet offshore. In several
different places I drop my dinghy anchor and snorkel. The water is quite shallow, from one to three feet, and I enjoy some interesting snorkeling. I see fish,
and an enormous hermit crab in a queen conch shell. I spot many barracudas, of all sizes, and many sea urchins and small corals. I snorkel into the
channels, and discover several pairs of romantic couples at the south end,
whom I leave alone. I find a small, empty beach , but except for this one patch
of sand the island is completely bordered by mangroves. With the trails it
does indeed look a bit like the island in the Gilligan's Island TV show. The
island is clearly very popular, with a ferry going back and forth almost continuously between here and the mainland.

The anchorage off Gilligan's Island is quiet. I get a good night's sleep. I leave at
6 in the morning, retracing my route through the cut through the reef. It is
always easier the second time.

Once in open water I discover that there are 6- to 8-foot seas, and about 20
knots of headwind for the trip to Ponce, about as predicted by NMN. Over
the last couple of weeks three fronts have developed. All have stalled out at

Hispaniola. If I wait for a front to give me winds from the west I may have to wait a long, long time. So I leave, and I decide to forget the sails, and motor direct. If I tack I will not make it before 11 o'clock, when the winds and seas begin to worsen.

I can make practically no headway with one engine, forcing me to double my fuel consumption for the 15-mile trip. I am very low on fuel. My last fuel stop was at Luperon several hundred miles ago, and since then I have been motoring continuously with an assist from the sail. I estimate that I will make it with fuel to spare. But the racket from two engines is more than double that from one, making the trip unpleasantly noisy.

And so I travel noisily into the sun and wind on a bouncy sea. As if that weren't enough, a significant current cuts into my speed. I arrive at Ponce on a wet boat, but I myself have managed — uncharacteristically — to remain dry. I head for the fuel dock at Ponce Yacht Club, an easy task. The dock is upwind, in deep water, and has good cleats. I come in as slowly as I can, and dock with no assistance. Two men show up and offer to get me fuel, but I decline until after I have called customs.

The yacht club is very busy. A large number of old people are dancing to Spanish music in one area, and the docks and surrounding area is full of younger people fishing with line and spindles. A local tells me a fishing contest for the handicapped is underway. I look for a phone far from the music and I call customs. After I satisfy them, they ask me to call agriculture, and then they put immigration on the line. Immigration decides to come over and see the boat and papers. Agriculture tells me not to bring any garbage ashore except plastic bottles and aluminum cans. Whatever crop pests or diseases I have on board must depart with me.

Now I try to get gas. The office says someone will be right over to serve me. The immigration man shows up, looks at the boat papers, and leaves. He is not interested in coming aboard to look around. I wait for my gas. Eventually, about an hour later, help arrives. I get my gas. The fuel dock is not busy, and apparently often unmanned.

The small area around the yacht club appears to be a popular anchorage. No sailboats are anchored outside the small harbor, and only about a dozen inside. I motor around the area and discover it is all about 30 feet deep. This makes me nervous since the boats are so close together, and the bottom, I am sure, is mud, not good holding. Furthermore, there is a 10- to 15-knot wind here. To get adequate scope I would need to put out over a 100 feet of rode. I don't want to swing into somebody if the wind changes. The other boats all appear to have chain rode, a big advantage in a tightly packed harbor since they need less scope than I do with only 40 feet of chain. They will also swing differently. I decide to put down an anchor to test the conditions. As soon as I have 80 feet of rode out I realize I will be too close to two other boats. Now I am nervous about pulling the anchor up and drifting into a neighboring boat, since I cannot be both at the helm and pulling the anchor up at the same time.

I consider using my anchor windlass. I usually do not use it, since it will only pull the rode, and not the chain. My chain is one size too big for the windlass. Furthermore, though my windlass is among the smallest made, it will still stress my modest electrical system. It will draw up to 100 amps of current under a moderate load, and under really stressing conditions it will not function at all. I decide not to use it since the 40 feet of chain will still reach the bottom.

Now, I implement a new strategy. I drag the anchor to a better position, being careful not to cross any other boat's anchor or chain. Using only one engine not much above idle, I find that I can easily drag the anchor parallel to the neighboring boats until I am well aft of them. The speed at which I do this is simultaneously satisfying and alarming. I am now in a much better spot, but I no longer have any faith that my anchor will hold. Still, without the engine on, I do not appear to be dragging the anchor. I let out another 40 feet of line. I have no close neighbors now, but am very close to two large buoys in the harbor. I carefully line up points on the shore so I can check to see if the boat is holding its position. Then I make lunch.

As I eat, I watch a tug bring in a U.S. Navy boat. After lunch I can detect no change in my position. I expect no storms tonight, and decide to let *Top Cat* be.

I head out after I eat for a walking tour of Ponce, the second largest city in Puerto Rico. Since this is a big city, I chain my dinghy to the fence. I start first for the U.S. Post Office. I am told it is only a 15-minute walk away. As I leave I am struck by the wealth represented in this yacht club. This could be Miami. I see many big expensive powerboats, and some beautiful sailboats, too. I look at one sailboat perilously perched on a trailer, and wonder how much water it would take to float that boat. If you did it using a truck, the truck would be under water! I suppose the trailer is used for land transport, not launching. The club also has a gate, and a guard at the gate

Outside the gate is a gigantic public park and a waterfront restaurants, all built by the city. It is popular, and there are many people here, with very loud music. Beer is sold at many of the veranda-style restaurants; outside vendors are selling food between the buildings

Ten minutes down the road I see a large marine store. I wander around inside for a while, but buy nothing. The clerk tells me the post office is 15 minutes away. I continue on, and in 10 minutes I arrive at a big, air-conditioned port building. People there tell me the post office is 15 minutes away. I begin to believe I am not going the direct route. I pass very nice residential areas, and

Outside the gate is a gigantic public park...

ask several people where the post office is. The language gap cannot be bridged, however. I continue on my way, expecting to find the post office at any moment. Here I find big roads, with cars everywhere. This place looks affluent. I talk to the guard at the large Hilton Hotel I pass. He tells me there is no post office. About a half hour later I run into a mail carrier, the same little USPS truck and uniform as in the states. He tells me the post office is far from here, too far for me to get to on foot. That's OK, I tell him, I am really just out for a walk. I turn down a dirt road next to a river. It leads to the ocean.

At the mouth of the river I come across a great view of Caja de Muertos, my destination for tomorrow. From here I see a beach to the west and the backside of the Hilton Hotel complex. People are clustered on the beach. Several are in the water up to their knees fishing. They have no fishing poles, but use the spooled fishing-line technique I see so often in Puerto Rico. As I walk by, one of them catches something big. Onlookers gather around him quickly. He steps out a little into the water and winds some of the line back up on the spindle. Then he walks backward, pulling the line and fish to shore. As it gets closer I can see that whatever it is, it is big.

Eventually he pulls it in. It is a large ray, perhaps 50 pounds. He gets help to gaff it and pull it up on the beach. They pull out the hook with vise-grip pliers, a relatively small hook compared to this big beast. Everybody is very excited about this catch and they all want me to take their pictures to record this event. Initially I refuse, but then I agree and take several pictures. The

It is a large ray, perhaps 50 pounds.

great beast struggles for life, and is still struggling when I leave about a half-hour later. I am sorry to witness the slow death of such a beautiful creature. But I do feel confident these people intend to eat it.

On my way back to the boat I stop at Rafa's Cash and Carry, a large warehouse store like Costco or Sam's back home and open to the public. It is about a half-mile from the yacht club, down the main road. I buy a turkey loaf for sandwiches, a few green peppers, and some cheese. The prices seem a little lower than U.S. prices, a first for this trip.

Arriving back at the yacht club, I am relieved to find that both the dinghy and *Top Cat* occupy the same spots they were in when I left for my walk. I have walked for about four hours, and I am tired. I decide to eat in.

A party goes on all Friday night around the yacht basin. There are hundreds of celebrants, and loud Latin music. I turn on the fan in my cabin, which produces considerable white noise, but not quite enough to drown out the revelry. I get up several times to check the anchor. We do not drag, but swing on our anchor to the north in unison with the other boats. During the night cool air slides down out of the mountains, giving all the anchorages on the mountainous south coast of Puerto Rico a light north wind. Between 4 and 5 in the morning the party finally winds down.

I get ready to leave at 6 o'clock. Even with only 10 knots of wind, I am concerned about a small drift with so little space between boats. I put both engines on in neutral, and with Otto disassembled I begin slowly to pull in the anchor. Once the anchor is clear of the bottom I move very quickly, hauling up the last 35 feet of chain and anchor like a speed demon. As I pull I notice I am now no more than 10 feet from my nearest neighbor. To my stern is a large barge with crane being used to build an addition to the dock, and to my other side a very large buoy used by the barge. I have little room to maneuver.

I get the anchor up, put a temporary line around it to hold it in place, and rush to the wheel. I turn the boat through 90 degrees using one engine forward, one reverse, and proceed to back out slowly. I am gasping for air from my exertions when my neighbor, drinking coffee on the deck of her boat just 20 feet away, calmly bids me good morning. With another disaster averted, I act totally in control as I exchange a few final pleasantries with her. She and her husband will leave shortly, going west to Boqueron. Once free of the tight confines of that harbor I vow to anchor next time in a great open space.

The lighthouse on the hilltop was built by Spain...

It is much calmer this morning. During the night the offshore breeze must have calmed the seas a bit. I motor directly into a 10-knot wind from the southeast.

I arrive at Caja de Muertos, a state park, before 8 o'clock and pick up a mooring. One large motor yacht is anchored, bow out, near shore. Otherwise the island's waters appear empty.

I leave for a walk. I climb to the lighthouse at the top of the hill. There are signs on the path in both Spanish and English. This is the first time I have seen a sign in English since arriving in Puerto Rico. One sign warns of a poisonous plant, and is surrounded by the poisonous plant. I discover that the path is lined with thorny brush and cactus plants. Too bad I am wearing shorts. I think I will christen this place Thorn Island. The lighthouse on the hilltop was built by Spain shortly before the United States gained possession of Puerto Rico more than a century ago. It is in poor condition. From the top looking west I can see the visitor center and the residence for the park rangers who live on Caja de Muertos.

From the top looking west I can see the visitor center...

I walk back down the hill and start out on the path to the eastern end of the island. It, too, is lined with thorny brush. There are lizards everywhere, but they are very shy. They scuttle off to hide as I approach. I see them in the dappled shadows of the thorn bushes. The birds, too, seem shy. I see them peeking out from behind branches, never perching out in the open.

...the path. is lined with thorny brush....

Nobody else is on the path, though about halfway down to the end of the island I hear what seems like a hundred people having a party right in front of me. I look and I look, but I see nobody. I look around again, and then I discover the source of the noise — a sailboat out on the water at least a half-mile away. Sound carries well here. I'm thinking that the sailboat carries one very happy group. Soon I will have company on the island. I make it all the way to the end of the island, and look out over the reefs. This is clearly a hazardous place for boating, but I'm willing to bet it's a fantastic snorkeling spot.

I head back to the boat for lunch, and then down to the visitor center. The visitor center is not impressive, with nothing more than a few posters to educate the visitor. But the grounds look good, with many covered picnic tables and a fine dock for a ferry that apparently is not now running. And now I see the boatload of happy people, on the beach near the visitor center!

I am surprised to discover that all of them are men, no women or children in the bunch. I talk to them. They speak good English. They are engineers from a local aerospace company. The boat is owned by one of the engineers, and they often come out here as a group. Most of them are in the water. One on the land is throwing drinks to them with great precision. They are amazingly

...and cactus plants.

noisy, producing at least as much noise as you would find among a group of the same size at a football game.

On my way back to the boat I stop by the little island in front of Caja de Muertos called Isla Morrilito. It is home to many birds, including the booby. I take a picture of these birds, but I get a little too close. Some of them start to dive-bomb me. Chastened, I head home to *Top Cat*.

It is home to many birds,including the booby.

I stop briefly for my snorkeling gear and then I am off again. Rounding the east end of the island in my dinghy, I encounter large swells and many exposed rocks over which they are crashing. I wend my way south carefully, standing up in the boat to watch for reefs. There are heads everywhere. I work my way toward one section of semi-exposed reef, then throw out the anchor. The water is moderately clear, and full of coral formations.

My dinghy drifts back over a huge brain coral. I swim out to move the anchor so that the rode does not damage it. Then I try to work my way up to some boat remains that are sticking out of the water. Getting there is not easy, and requires me to swim over fire coral in about six inches of water. I suck in my stomach. The wreck is scattered all over this shallow reef. I don't doubt that it is one of many in this reef-strewn area.

Making my way back home out of this minefield is not easy. Even standing in the boat so I have a clear look ahead, and moving cautiously, I am frequently surprised by a head. The water breaks over some, while others lurk six inches under the water. Between the heads the water is anywhere from two to six feet deep. I see another small boat come, and then go. It, too, moves slowly, with two men on the bow watching for heads while a third steers.

Back at *Top Cat* I have my drink and dinner. As I drink the boatload of happy engineers comes by on their way home. They all wave and shout. I take their picture.

They all wave and shout. I take their picture.

I make some cell phone calls. I find my cell phone works everywhere in Puerto Rico, as it did in much of the Bahamas. I use a calling card and am able to complete my calls without operator intervention. In the Bahamas I had to first pay $21 per week for roaming privileges to Batelco, the Bahamas Telecommunications Corporation, then I dialed direct without a calling card. I have a long conversation with my son, and call the Crown Bay Marina in St. Thomas to reserve a slip there for the day my wife comes in.

After a good night's sleep I head out at 6 o'clock Sunday morning for Salinas. I motor the entire 15-mile distance into a 10-knot headwind. I arrive around 9, and anchor just south of the crowd of boats in the harbor. Some boats are exceedingly tightly packed, but I am on the outskirts of the anchorage, with one anchor out, and I feel secure here.

I turn on the VHF and listen to the cruiser gossip before I depart for some sightseeing. One cruiser talks to another about the new set of batteries he has just installed that don't seem to be working well. He wants to leave, and is not sure if he should return the batteries and go back to his old ones before his departure. Another talks about relatives arriving next week and the need to remain here for another few weeks to entertain these visitors. A third cruiser talks about a friend who is working on getting rid of fishing net caught in his propeller so he can leave today. The net, I gather, has been there for some time. Next, I hear a tug call the cruiser with the fouled prop. The cruiser has anchored in the channel to a nearby refinery and the tug pilot says he draws 20 feet and wants to proceed through the channel. The cruiser says he has some fishing net caught in his propeller and is working to remove it. I wonder why he had to anchor in the channel. Couldn't he drift or sail out of the channel so he wouldn't impede travel through it? I suspect incompetence on the part of the cruiser. This story develops like something in a soap opera. I decide not to stay for the next episode, but to set out for some sightseeing in my dinghy.

I visit the Cayos de Ratones, directly to the south, and look at the surf breaking over the reef behind it. I see some pelicans, and I take their picture, as well as one of the tug and barge from the VHF soap opera a mile or so off the coast. They are circling out there, obviously forced to wait until the cruiser leaves.

I head off to look for beaches. There are few, and they are small. Most of the shore is lined with mangroves. I explore some mangrove creeks in my dinghy. According to one of my guidebooks, these are black mangroves. They can be identified by their arching roots and encrusting oysters.

They are circling out there...

Back at the boat, I have lunch. I am amazed at all the local traffic going back and forth. Jetskiers speed up and down the channel, ignoring the sign in mid-channel warning of manatees. Long cigarette boats with double 250-horse-power outboards zoom by, and many sportfishing boats with inboards rumble past. I see dozens of powerboats in the 18- to 25-foot range. The powerboats are generally teeming with people, six to ten of them aboard most. And I see the *Policia*! I have seen a number of these boats since arriving in Puerto Rico, while I never saw one in the Dominican Republic or the Bahamas. One of them stops three boats all at once right in front of me: two jetskis and one small powerboat. The three policemen on board spend 10 minutes giving out tickets. Maybe the traffic will slow down for a bit.

The Salinas harbor is surrounded by mangroves, and is comparable in size to the harbor at Luperon. The many mangrove creeks here make excellent hurricane holes. The water here is no clearer than at Luperon; in both harbors, the water is clouded by silt washed from the land. The bottom here probably has a little more sand than mud compared to Luperon, resulting in better holding for anchoring.

I spend the afternoon talking to cruisers. There is a large contingent of cruisers here who live permanently on their boats, similar to the large number of cruisers who live on boats in George Town, Great Exuma. Perhaps as many as a third of the fifty cruising families here now in Salinas are permanent residents. They pay no rent or property taxes. One works at the marina, another is the warden of a nearby private prison, and a third does odd jobs, including

The Salinas harbor...is comparable in size to the harbor at Luperon.

cleaning the bottoms of boats in the harbor. But most do not work. One I talk to is 83, another is 72; these two don't have much interest in going anywhere else.

Some boats are here permanently, but the people who own them are not. Cruisers I talk to point out boats that are the equivalent of second homes: they have occupants only about half the year. Some cruisers spend most of their time here, but do go on occasional trips. One popular destination is Venezuela. Some go south to Venezuela every couple of years to have their boats hauled and painted and to load up on supplies. The cost of food and other items is relatively cheaper there, I am told. Marinas in Venezuela also use a more durable bottom paint than the environmental regulations allow in the United States or Puerto Rico.

Until the early 1990s relatively few cruisers came to Salinas. Then, as word of the advantages of the harbor spread, more and more cruisers came. And, as more cruisers came, cruiser services popped up in the small town of Playa Salinas. Now there are mail services, general office services, weather reports, boat watching services, restaurants, marine hardware, sailmakers, food stores, good transportation, and much more. The local stores hand out maps, and business and store owners speak English. The marina sponsors a potluck dinner for cruisers on Monday nights and a barbecue on Fridays. The harbor is very popular with the Puerto Rican locals on the weekends, but is pretty much owned by the cruisers on the weekdays.

The growth has annoyed some longtime cruisers. They complain about the floodlights turned on in front of a local waterside restaurant. These floodlights are so bright that it is difficult to see the stars at night. The place is beginning to resemble a suburban community. Some of the cruisers also suspect that drug traffic is picking up locally.

The cruising life has been contentious for some families here. One boat is owned by a divorcee, part of her divorce settlement. Another boat is owned by a divorced man who got it when he and his wife separated; he is now on his second wife. Very often the boat is the major asset owned by a cruiser family. It is usually the woman who has the most trouble with cruising. One woman cruiser told me about a study of women cruisers. She said the study showed that a good predictor of whether a woman would like cruising was the degree to which she participated in and enjoyed camping when she was young. Those who hated camping were unlikely to enjoy cruising.

Many aspects of the cruising life do resemble camping. We are self-contained and we travel light. We often have to make do. We conserve everything. Most of us have no TV or major household appliances aboard. The woman who told me about the study of women cruisers said that her daughter gives her a hard time when she visits because she won't use her daughter's dishwasher. She says she read the directions, and discovered that the dishwasher uses 15 gallons of water for each load! This cruiser just couldn't imagine using so many precious gallons of fresh water to wash dishes.

At dusk I see, hear, and feel mosquitoes. What can one expect with so much standing water back in the mangroves? That is the down side of the protection provided by mangrove creeks. One cruiser told me that when hurricane Hortense came through in September 1996, cruisers here sheltered their boats back in the mangrove creeks by tying the ship's bow to the mangroves and throwing an anchor off the stern. They sustained no damage from the hurricane's 80-knot winds. Between hurricane seasons, however, the mosquitoes provide a reason to be elsewhere. When the tradewinds die, they come out to visit the boats and feed. I go inside and put my screens up, and that is the end of that. I also put my anchor light on. Then later, very much later, I note that nobody else here has an anchor light on. Not one other boat!

In the morning I dinghy in and walk to town. It is about a half-hour walk, and is hot. The town has a very distinct Latin flavor. All the signs are in Spanish, and the songs I hear are in Spanish. The local kids love to drive down the street with their radios on as loud, I am sure, as they can go. I discover that there is rap in Spanish! But the post office could be in Florida, and the supermarket is just like the one at home. There are also Cash and Carry warehouse stores, as in Ponce. Apparently these are everywhere in Puerto Rico. I am told that when food stamps are sent out each month these stores are packed.

I do a few chores in town. I drop letters off at the post office and I pick up some fresh vegetables at the supermarket. I do my laundry at the marina, fill up on propane, and stop at the Playa Salinas bakery. The pastries look and taste good. I buy four different freshly baked delicacies. The coconut ones are great, but I am stuffed after eating the first.

In the morning I am up at 6 o'clock and drive *Top Cat* over to the mangrove bayou next to Jobos. I put down the anchor not far off the channel so that I can leave rapidly on Wednesday for the east coast. I want to explore this place by dinghy. It is claimed by some to be the best hurricane hole in the Caribbean.

I motor slowly in the dinghy because this is a manatee sanctuary. I have been told that the locals used to eat the manatees. I notice that some local boats are moving much faster than me, and that a *Policia* boat just went by heading east

The channels appear to be deep...right up to the mangroves.

going 30 knots, at least! I am tempted to speed up, but instead I proceed sedately northwest, into the maze of mangrove-lined waterways.

I travel past a series of open water basins, or bayous, connected by narrow channels. Here one can tie the bow and stern off to mangroves on either side of the channel: no anchors are needed. The channels are deep, perhaps 6 feet or so, right up to the mangroves. This is a good hurricane hole, though not as large as the system of mangrove creeks off the Shark River in the Everglades.

I find no houses back here, only an occasional fishing boat. Finally I reach the end of the series of basins, where I find a settlement. These people have a long way to go to get to open water, but they are doubtless safer from big storms than those who live near the harbor.

I leave early Wednesday morning, April 29, bound for Cayo Santiago, despite a discouraging weather report. Last night's Perfect Paul forecast predicted winds northeast to east at 15 to 20 knots, with no change over the next several days. Tuesday night he predicted east winds at 15 to 20 knots with no change over the next several days. He seems to be predicting steadily deteriorating conditions as far as my trip plans are concerned. Should I believe him, despite his inability to stick with his forecast? I must have faith in him since he is my only source of information.   I also realize that his prediction is for the open water. The wind is blocked by the mountains and channeled around this coast and, just as current in a stream picks up speed when the stream narrows, I expect a stronger wind near this coast. It will be even worse with a northeast wind. I am not willing to wait four days in the hope of better weather.

This will be a long trip compared with my recent short hops: 33 nautical miles. Van Sant makes the next stop at Puerto Patillas, but the place does not interest me today. Furthermore, I would like to reach Puerto del Rey early tomorrow. I pass out of Boca de Infierno, a very scary name, at first light. To do this I rise at 4:30, reassemble Otto, put up the sail with one reef, pull up the anchor, and go. I am at the cut by 5:45. I see breakers to the left and to the right, just as the sun is coming up. The opening is much smaller than I thought. I see rocks out of the water 100 feet to the left, and breakers to the right. But I have aligned the chimneys on land, as shown on the chart, and am at the correct GPS location. My depth meter shows no shallow water.

Once out, I am in big waves, maybe eight to ten feet. It is early in the morning and already it is very bouncy. I have closed all the hatches in preparation for

I ...put up the sail with one reef...

just such conditions. It gets worse. The wind is now on the nose, the sun is in my eyes, the current is against me and strong, and I see floats! I really hate floats. These look particularly lethal. They are multiple plastic bottles, or a bottle and two styrofoam floats, or three styrofoam floats. Between the floats are floating lines. If I pass over one of them I am sure to get my engine entangled. Watching for floats will keep me awake, as if anybody could sleep on this bouncy boat.

I take down the sail. There's no change of speed; the sail is no help at all. With only one engine I am making only a couple of knots. I turn on the second engine. I need more power to reach my destination before sundown.

As I get to Punta Figuras the sea calms a bit, but with the Guayama Reef to starboard, my GPS loses convergence. This is not Geeps's fault. Geeps has a number of satellites in view, but their relative positions are such that he cannot solve the equations to determine our position. I have no doubt that this problem will shortly be overcome since both my boat and the satellites are on the move. I watch the breakers to my right and left, and continue on. Within 10 minutes, Geeps has accumulated needed information and is providing me with constantly updated positions.

At Puerta Patillas I am able to cut one engine and put the sail up. We pick up speed. I have about 20 knots of apparent wind, and am doing about 4 knots. As I round Punta Tuna at 9:30 I learn what strong tradewinds can do. One moment the apparent wind is 22 knots. The next it is 32 knots. And the seas have doubled in size! The real wind is over 25 knots. It is coming directly from where I am going! In seconds I am thoroughly soaked with spray. Nothing on the outside of this boat remains dry. Luckily, I have the sail up. Without the sail I would be going backward! With the sail I can make some forward progress by dropping off to starboard, but it is exceedingly slow going because of the very rough seas. The bow reaches to the sky, then slams down. We roll left, then right. Spray is everywhere. I head off the wind more to reduce the slamming. Now we are headed well offshore.

After an hour, the seas are a little calmer, the apparent wind is down a bit, but we are far off our target. I will continue on this tack until our destination is directly north. Then I will tack to port.

I make lunch, thankful for the narrowness of my little galley. I can wedge myself in to make my sandwich. The boat is bouncing so much that carrying my sandwich from the galley to the helm is tricky, yet I want to eat outside. Outside I am less likely to be seasick, and I also feel like I am taking a hand in my forward progress, though with Geeps in charge of navigation, Otto at the helm, the sail up, and the engines on, I am not, in truth, doing much of anything at all.

Otto is performing well. The boat is roughly in balance. This is achieved with the reefed main pulled in relatively tight and the starboard engine on. If I used the port engine, Otto would loose control because the mainsail alone, without the jib, provides a torque to the boat that moves it around and into the wind. The starboard engine provides a torque in the opposite direction. By balancing engine and sail, I allow Otto to steer despite strong winds. With a weak autopilot like Otto, the boat must be roughly in balance for the autopilot to work effectively.

When Cayo Santiago is due north I come about through the wind and seas to a starboard tack. Sailing is better on this tack, since the rollers seem to be from the east (where the wind as been in previous days) while the wind is from the northeast as correctly predicted by Perfect Paul.

It is a long trip, but by 4 o'clock I have arrived. This is Cayo Santiago, Monkey Island, a free range for the Caribbean Primate Research Center.

Naturally, I have made up my mind to go look for the monkeys.

This is Cayo Santiago, Monkey Island...

I anchor in 12 feet of water, and dive on the anchor. I see 22 knots of real wind on my instruments and I observe a very strong pull on the anchor. I put out my 40 feet of chain and another 70 feet of rode. I wonder if there is coral down there. Could it chafe my rode? I need to look. I put on my snorkeling equipment and dive on the anchor. I see a lovely grass-and-sand bottom, no coral. The anchor is set well. I will sleep tonight.

I dinghy to the island to check out the primates. Signs warn me against landing here. I find no good beaches, and this side of the island is very shoal. I drift up and down the shore looking for monkeys, and do see a couple, but from quite a distance.

I drift up and down the shore looking for monkeys, and I do see a couple...

Key Lois, a tiny island near my home port, has been used as a home for a breeding colony of rhesus monkeys in recent years. The monkeys are used in laboratory research. For a time they had the run of the island and their lives were wild and free, but environmental groups, both government and private, became concerned about the damage they were doing to the island's mangroves and the tons of waste they produced that inevitably ended up in the ocean. Now their free-ranging days are over. They are all enclosed in huge open-air cages on the island, and the breeders are busy planting mangrove seedlings to replace those lost to monkey destruction. The monkeys themselves have been evicted and will eventually be moved to other homes. Such is life. Score one for the environment, zero for the monkeys.

There is nobody here but me and some jetskiers. Two come by from the nearby marina, doing tricks, falling off their jetskis, while I am out in the cockpit taking my shower. If they wanted excitement they should have been with me today in the waves and wind.

After sunset I see the headlights of cars moving up and down the coast.

I wake at 5:15 and I am underway in half an hour, at sunrise. The seas are not bad, and the wind is about 16 knots. I go directly into the wind, and use both engines. The apparent wind is over 20 knots for most of the morning. A few times I hit the seas badly, and the boat is drenched. On one of these occasions, the salon is thoroughly doused, as well.

By 9 o'clock I am at Isla Pineros, and I am able to head northwest to Puerto del Rey. I decide to stop at Puerto del Rey Marina because it is the largest marina in the Caribbean basin, and I want to see something big. I'd like to know if there are many cruisers who stay at marinas. Also, I am well ahead of schedule, and will take a couple days to see the sights.

This is a big marina, supposedly 750 slips. I call the harbormaster on VHF, and ask for help getting into a transient slip. I come upwind into my slip, and with two dock hands to help me I have no trouble. The dock is concrete and about two feet above my rub rail. I am downwind, and will probably never touch it, but I put out bumpers just to be safe.

I already understand the disadvantages of big marinas: here, as at other big marinas I have visited, it is a long walk to the office. I get a ride on a golf cart this time. Golf carts seem to be everywhere, driven by staff, not boaters. At the office I pay a dollar per foot per day for the transient slip. I also rent a car for $30 per day.

I go back to the boat to use some of the free fresh water. I cannot relate to the woman in Salinas who didn't like using water. I flood the boat with fresh water, enjoy watching it sheet down over the hatches, brightwork, and hull, and drip off. I feel good. Everything is rinsed and salt-free.

In my rental car, I set out for the Caribbean National Forest, known as El Yunque. It is the only tropical rain forest administered by the U.S. National Forest Service. I have no directions, but I am given a map. It soon occurs to me that on this small island, about 100 miles long and 50 miles wide, it is hard to get lost and easy to find a place if you just drive around for a while. Within a half-hour I am at the rain forest.

The visitor center is beautiful, surrounded by rain forest. It consists of very high roofed structures without enclosing walls. There is a background of bird noises and a strong sense of vertical space. I watch the orientation film presented alternately in English and Spanish. There are few people at the center.

Next I head up the mountain. It is indeed a good example of the tropical rain forest. A light rain is falling around me. The foliage is lush and green. I talk to a couple of guys from Los Angeles who visited the Costa Rican rain forest last year; this one is more lush, they say, except that there they saw birds. Here the birds hide from view. I hear the sounds of birds, frogs, and crickets, but I don't see them.. The rain forest is dark. I find it difficult to take pictures

I go on about half the walks, and spend four or five hours walking. It is good exercise and I enjoy the afternoon. On the way back I stop at one of the large Cash and Carry warehouse grocery stores for a few supplies. All the large U.S. chains seem to be represented here. I pass Kmart, Walmart, Target, Walgreens, Burger King, McDonalds, Checkers, and many more. I do not see U.S. automobile sales centers but many Japanese and Korean automobile car lots.

Back at the marina I spend the evening walking around and talking to cruisers about cruising. The vast majority of the sailboats here are charter boats and there are hundreds of them. There are many more powerboats than sailboats, and many of them are for charter, too. The sailboats here are bigger and the cruisers appear to be more affluent on average than at Salinas or George Town. At the high end is an 84-foot ketch manned by a crew of three. They are en route to the owner, who awaits his boat in Rhode Island. The owner, who lives in England, flies over to sail for a week or so every month or two. The real cruiser here is the captain of the ketch, who cruises with his wife and has help from two deckhands. He gets paid for it. I found it interesting that the captain had just consulted with Herb, as do so many. Herb told him that conditions were not right to sail for Rhode Island in the morning, so they are waiting at the marina for the weather to improve.

A different style of part-time cruising is represented by a couple on a 47-foot sloop who sailed down from Vancouver, Canada. They own a business there, and are able to cruise only part-time. Because of time constraints they generally travel straight through. I told them that I made the trip from Florida in only five weeks. They told me they generally make that trip in five days! They travel day and night, around the clock. They don't stop. And the trip from Canada, through the Panama Canal? It took them two months this time.

I talked to a cruising couple who work at the marina and live on their boat. They cruised for 13 years in the Caribbean but got a job here after their trimaran was capsized and badly damaged in hurricane Hugo a few years ago. Now they are planning to cruise only half the year, working at the marina the other half. They have just bought some farmland nearby, and are considering building a house. In true cruiser style they plan to build a self-sufficient farmhouse and use solar panels for power. They have lived for decades without utilities, so why would they need them now?

In the morning I drive to Old San Juan. I visit the forts, the churches, the mansions, the gates, and the congested city. I walk everywhere, and get plenty of exercise. On the way back I stop at some small towns. The disparity between rich and poor here is striking. There is grandeur and there is also decay. I am astonished by the poor condition of waterfront buildings in many small towns, such as in Fajardo. I do not believe that waterfront property in Puerto Rico is nearly so highly valued as it is in the States.

In the later afternoon I return the car and inform the marina I will be leaving early in the morning. I pick up a golf-cart ride back to the boat.

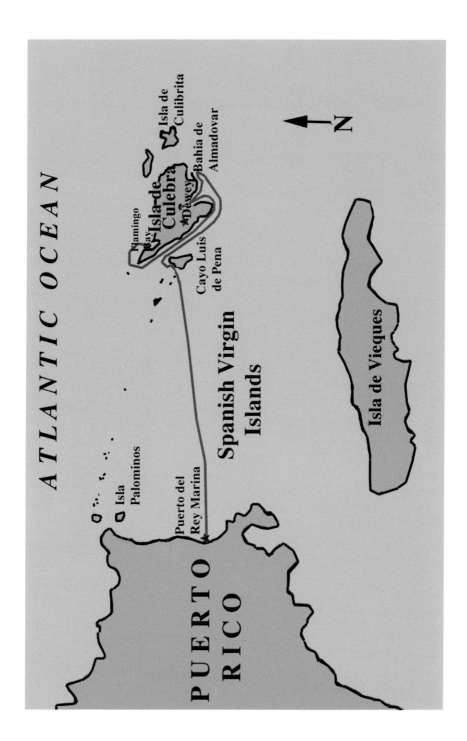

7: The Spanish Virgin Islands

In the morning I set out at 6 o'clock for Isla Palominos, a very short and easy trip, on my way to the Spanish Virgin Islands. Once out of the harbor, however, I am impressed by the relative quiet of the sea, and decide to go straight to Cayo de Luis Pena, off Culebra. I motor directly there in 2- to 4-foot seas and against 10 knots of headwind. I use both engines out of fear that the conditions will change before I arrive. They don't, and I get there by 9 o'clock.

These islands are part of the Commonwealth of Puerto Rico, and have a Spanish heritage. They have far fewer people than the U.S. and British Virgin Islands and are almost totally ignored by tourists. Still, I see plenty of cruisers through here, if for no other reason than they are on the way to the islands to the east.

Cayo de Luis Pena is paradise, and I am alone. Beautiful water, reefs, and beach. I walk the beach, climb over the rocks, snorkel a little, and relax. I marvel at the color variations in the rocks.

Just before lunch a seaplane arrives and parks right next to my dinghy. It is a plane, complete with pilot, rented by a couple on their honeymoon. They have come to paradise for the afternoon. Later several powerboats from Puerto Rico arrive.

This area is full of small uninhabited rock islands. I explore some of them by dinghy. Most appear to be protected bird habitat, but not all have birds. Over one of the islands the birds continually swarm, like bees around a hive.

Late in the afternoon I motor to the south of Culebra and anchor at Bahia de Almodovar. The anchorage at Luis Pena was not bad, but there is a north swell today that I escape at my new spot. This harbor is protected to the south by a reef, and to the north by mangroves. There is no roll, and the water is very quiet. Several other sailboats, and eight or so powerboats, share my anchorage. From here I can see St. Thomas, USVI, only 18 nautical miles away.

In the morning I snorkel the shallow reef. I swim in one to four feet of water just north of the breaking waves. It is quiet water, and beautiful snorkeling, with a wide variety of aquatic life in a number of different kinds of habitats. I see clear sand bottom areas, areas with a variety of sea grasses, and isolated pockets of coral formations surrounded by colorful fish.

In the afternoon I dinghy over to the east side of Culebra and find a beach accessible only through a cut in a reef. Only a small, shallow-draft boat like my dinghy can make it through. I take a long walk, perhaps a mile. I interrupt a mother bird protecting her nest. I encounter a crab that first threatens me, then buries itself. It is a pleasant walk. The sand is well-packed underfoot, easier to walk on than the fluffy beach at Luis Pena, but not hard enough or pretty enough to be a first-rate beach for running.

Later I cross the Canal de Culebrita to Isla de Culebrita, and follow the path to the lighthouse at the top. The lighthouse dates from the 1800s, and is not in service. The entrance through the reefs requires a steady hand at the tiller and a careful watch. The path to the island's peak is not too warm today but I imagine that it will be blazing come August. This is a desert-like environment, with lots of cacti. The views are fantastic. The Culebrita reef is clearly visible

The views are fantastic.

miles out to sea. My anchorage is in the west, and I can see *Top Cat*. To the north I see the beach at the north end of Culebrita I plan to visit soon. There are several sailboats there today.

...I encounter a hummingbird and attempt to take its picture.

On the way back I encounter a hummingbird and attempt to take its picture. It moves swiftly so I must work hard to capture it on film.

I dinghy back to *Top Cat* for some water, then out to the near reef. I do what my wife and I frequently do in the Keys. I go upwind in the dinghy, then pull up the engine and drift back over the shallow water, watching the bottom. The water is very clear. I drift over many different kinds of bottom life: many coral communities, grasses, white sandy bottoms, and then I am into the mangroves. I drift for half and hour or so, and really enjoy it.

Back at the boat I plan how I will spend a few days in Culebra before heading for St. Thomas.

In the morning I motor to Dewey, the only city on Culebra. I find a bulldozer busy building a road and I see many expensive homes. A number of very large houses are here, probably serving as retreats for wealthy Puerto Ricans.

I anchor off the west side of Cayo Pirata in Ensenado Honda, very near to town. I lower the dinghy, and climb into it to motor under the bridge and out the channel to Bahia de Sardinas, which is open to the sea on the west side of Culebra. Just a few cruisers are anchored here today. I dinghy back to the other side, spotting no dinghy docks along the channel. I find a dinghy dock at a marina, and another one at the Dinghy Dock Restaurant (had to be one there, right?). I stop at the restaurant, and take a walk around the small town. I head for the post office to mail some letters, then to a grocery store to pick up some supplies. The town is small, but charming, with buildings painted in

...a dinghy dock.... at the Dinghy Dock Restaurant...

bright colors, and is mostly built on the side of a hill. I consider staying for the afternoon and having dinner at the restaurant, which has tables outside over-looking Ensenado Honda. But there are no nearby beaches to walk, so I pull up my anchor and head for Flamingo Beach on the north side of the island. This is the town beach, and must be the nicest beach in the Spanish Virgin Islands.

I motor-sail with the jib rolled open, without Otto or Geeps, since I am too lazy to go to the trouble of hoisting the main for such a short trip. (I have come to view anything under 15 miles as a short trip.) The ride is very pretty, past many small rocky islets.

I proceed into Flamingo Bay by sight alone, keeping clear of the reefs on both sides. The reef to the west is most extensive, but can easily be located from the seas breaking over it. A dozen dolphins continually cross in front of me. They are fun to watch in the clear waters of the bay. I move close to the beach and anchor in 25 feet of water just outside the small buoys marking the swimming area. I dive on my anchor; it is held securely in a sandy bottom. A northerly swell rumples the bay waters, resulting in surf on the beach, a rolling motion on *Top Cat*, and the total absence of cruisers. The surf no doubt contributes to the building of this beautiful beach, so I find it hard to be critical.

I...anchor...just outside the small buoys marking the swimming area.

I dinghy around and look for a safe place to reach shore. The only suitable spot appears to be at the east end, on the other side of a shallow reef. I approach the reef, then cut my engine and pull it out of the water. I drift and paddle over a magnificent reef, just inches to a couple of feet below the water. I pull the boat up on the rocky beach at the extreme east end of Flamingo Beach, and tie the painter to a tree.

This beach has real dunes, and a wide expanse of very white sand. It is empty today. I see a hotel, complete with beach chairs but no people. Now for some exercise. Can I run? The beach is fine, but too fluffy be a first-rate running beach. I walk instead.

I am now able to pick up the VHF weather channel from St. Thomas. It is continuous so I can listen anytime I want. It is all in English, whereas the VHF weather channel out of San Juan alternates between English and Spanish, and I am always missing the English part due to inattention. And, while San Juan provides only the coastal reports, St. Thomas also reads the NMN offshore reports. The offshore report tonight indicates no change in conditions, and none expected for the next 18 hours. I should have 15 knots of wind out of the southeast. I decide to head out in the morning for St. Thomas.

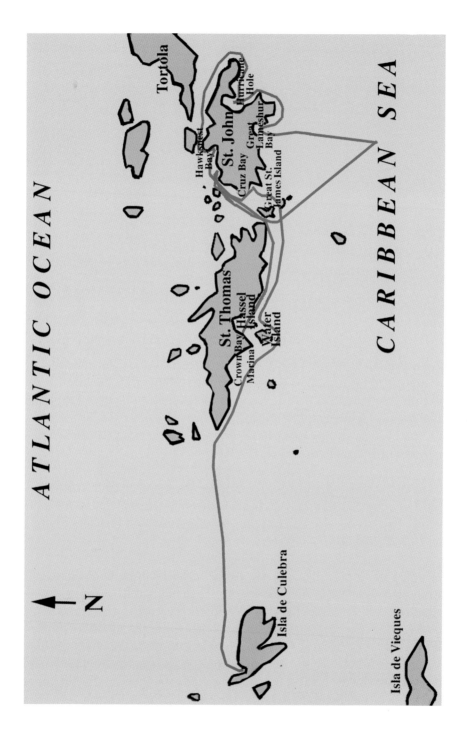

8: The U.S. Virgin Islands

At 6 in the morning I leave for St. Thomas, motoring out of the bay into a rolly sea. Once out of the bay I reassemble Otto and I put up the mainsail. With the wind out of the southeast I can head for the north side of St. Thomas and gain considerable assistance from the main. Later in the morning the wind seems to go a bit further south, so I pull out the jib and cut the engine. Then, after an hour, it moves eastward again, and I turn on the engine and pull in the flapping jib. I keep my speed at about 4 knots, and set my bearing to Dutchcap Cay off the northwest coast of St. Thomas. It is a slow and bouncy trip in 4- to 6-foot waves, with some spray.

At Dutchcap I tack until I am able to make the Savana Passage. The seas on the outside of Savana Island appear to be worse, so I opt to stay closer to St. Thomas. I begin to see sailboats. One is sailing, but most are motoring. I, too, drop my main, and motor directly into the wind, now coming down the side of St. Thomas, mainly from the east.

I look for an anchorage on the west side of Water Island within a mile or so of Charlotte Amalie harbor. It is jammed with boats all along the channel. Most of the boats are anchored in 30 feet of water or more, packed tightly. I stop at a couple of places, and motor between boats, considering anchoring. Each time I prepare to drop the hook I have second thoughts. I don't feel comfortable anchoring so close to other boats in water so deep.

I continue around the other side of the island, between Water and Hassel Islands. I find no sailboats here. The bottom appears to be more rock than sand, and there is less sea room.

Rounding the south end of Hassel Island, I see the handsome and enormous Mariott Hotel rising above the hill to the east. I head north toward Charlotte Amalie Harbor. It is full of boats. I anchor with one anchor in 20 feet of water at the end of the pack, just east of Kings Wharf. There is a roll, but I suspect there is a roll everywhere in this harbor. I have room around me! I have reached my destination, and I am twelve whole days early! I will see St. Thomas and St. John, but leave the rest until my wife arrives.

I take a tour of the harbor in my dinghy, discovering two big dinghy docks, one at Yacht Haven Marina at the east end, and one at Crown Bay Marina on the west end. Both docks are close to stores and restaurants.

I take a tour of the harbor...

This is a very busy harbor. I spend much of the late afternoon being entertained by the boats and planes. The international airport is just to the west of Crown Bay Marina, and is constantly busy, with planes taking off and arriving. Seaplanes take off from the harbor not far from my boat. A hydrofoil, looking like a gigantic spider supported on struts many feet out of the water, comes into the harbor. It settles back down on its haunches to take on the look of an ordinary boat before docking. Big, broad-beamed party boats roar by, their on-deck MCs loudly coaxing customers into dancing around the deck and singing together. Helicopters dart every which way.

I most like watching the giant cruise ships. These colossal boats manage to get in and out of here with only the assistance of a single small pilot boat. To leave they back directly into the channel, then turn 90 degrees in place using bow thrusters. They seem to perfectly align themselves with the channel, then head straight out, with half the passengers on deck watching, doubtless just as impressed as I am by this display of maritime virtuosity. Two ships are docked when I arrive, the Nordic Express and the Sensation, and both leave late in the afternoon, one going east, and one going west.

I most like watching the giant cruise ships.

I leave in the morning as another cruise ship approaches from the west. I try not to get in its way as I head east into the waves, current, wind, and sun. I motorsail, but am tempted to drop sail and just motor. Most sailboats I pass are motoring, even those headed west! I sail through Current Hole, and into Pillsbury Sound, headed for Cruz Bay on St. John.

I lower my main off Cruz Bay and motor in. I tour the bay looking for an acceptable anchorage. The boats are on top of each other and they are anchored in 20 to 30 feet of water! Fortunately there is little current. But there are numerous ferries that go back and forth between here and Red Hook on St. Thomas and the waves from their wake are more or less continuous. This is a very busy harbor. I wonder what would happen if a ferry comes by during the time I am pulling up 30 feet of chain and my anchor on my way out. I need about a minute to do this, and during this time there is nobody at the helm. *Top Cat* could be pushed by a wake into a boat just a few feet away, or drift back in a wind gust. No anchorage in Cruz Bay today, I decide, and turn my boat to head north. Boats are anchored everywhere along the coast as I travel north. I turn in to look for a spot at several places, but can't find a place with enough room in less than 40 feet of water. Finally I find a place in Caneel Bay with 30 feet of water, and nobody downwind of me. Here I can drift backward in relative safety as I haul up my anchor.

The dinghy ride back to Cruz Bay only takes five minutes in my fast dinghy. I decide to avoid crowded anchorages entirely, anchor on the fringes, and depend on my dinghy for transportation. This place is so small I could dinghy around the entire island.

My first stop is at the National Park Service Virgin Islands Visitor Center. I pick up a brochure on the park, which covers most of St. John, and I pick up a schedule of park events. The exhibits are not very extensive, and everything is in one room. The visitor center will shortly be expanded, I am told.

The streets around the bay are crowded, then relatively empty, as the ferry-boats come and go. I discover many shops, and a grocery store where I buy some tomatoes. I have lunch at an outdoor restaurant.

Returning to *Top Cat*, I decide to move to a better anchorage on the northwest side of St. John, one with even fewer people, and then to dinghy to shore. I motor a couple of miles up the coast to Francis Bay, probably the most protected anchorage on this side of the island. Only one other boat is at anchor here, perhaps because the guidebook says this spot can be buggy. I anchor in 20 feet of water on sand. I dive on my anchor and discover that, while there is sand everywhere else, the spot where my anchor has come to is marked by a large boulder. If I pull the chain from the south it will have to move the bolder to wrench free. This is good to know. I am pleased that I have finally collected some useful information by diving on my anchor.

I dinghy to Cinnamon Bay, about a mile or so to the south, and snorkel around Cinnamon Cay, where there is an underwater trail. I see many reef fish among the corals that cover the drowned granite boulders that clutter the roots of the cay. Later, I walk the beach, filled with vacationers who have come by plane. They are almost as colorful as the underwater world a few tens of feet away. Some sport really fine sunburns, the sure sign of a tourist. You can easily reach Cinnamon Cay from the beach, so many of the tourists snorkel here.

Back at *Top Cat* I watch from the deck as the boat is surrounded by a large school of yellow grunts feasting on a school of tiny fish. The splashing of predator and prey attracts the birds, who eat too. All this is within a few yards of the boat, and in crystal-clear water.

I talk to my neighbor, who I had assumed was a cruiser since he is on an uncommon boat with no charter company name emblazoned on the side or on the sail cover. I discover that I was wrong. He is, in fact, a charter boater. He mentions that the boat has a broken block, but he isn't concerned. He has decided not to sail! I can understand his decision, since the typical trip among the Virgins can probably be accomplished in a hour of motoring. Why fuss with the sail?

...clusters of pink flowers, where giant black bees hover.

In the morning there are clouds, but no wind. I take the Francis Bay Trail marked on the park map. It is a pretty walk up the hill past old plantation ruins. I see more hummingbirds, and fail again to get a good picture. While I am taking a picture of a yellow flower a hummingbird zips in, sips his nectar, and departs before I can snap the shutter.

The trees here are draped with vines covered with clusters of pink flowers, where giant black bees hover. They move faster than hummingbirds, and I find it hard to get a good picture of a black bee, too. I keep trying, hoping I'll get a good picture purely by accident.

The trail winds through a salt pond, a very shallow body of salty water. Here again I see birds, many more than in Puerto Rico.

In the afternoon I go over to Trunk Bay where the National Park Service maintains an underwater snorkeling trail marked with signs. I count about 10 signs and find that the trail is much shorter and not as interesting as the one around Cinnamon Cay. It is obviously geared to the novice snorkeler. Many pasty-white tourists are here, dog-paddling around.

I have been here two nights. I have called my wife and children. I am pleased that I am back in touch, delighted that my cell phone works here as it did in the Bahamas, though here I must use a credit card or calling card. I decide I really have nowhere I need to go, so stay yet a third night. Tomorrow I will do some boat chores.

The morning is very calm. A low has moved in and restrained the tradewinds for a day. I decide to climb the mast to remove one of the two antennas I installed for the SSB receiver. This wire parallels the mast, and resonates when the wind is strong and the sail is up next to it on a starboard tack. The wire has stretched, allowing it to resonate in large-amplitude standing waves big enough to hit the sail. The waves, usually three complete waves, are interesting to watch, but I worry about potential damage to the sail. My other antenna wire is connected at one end to the lifeline, and raised to the top of the mast by means of the spinnaker halyard.

I climb a ladder pulled up by the main halyard. It is composed of PVC pipe for rungs, and nylon ribbing. I have been up to the top of the mast a few times before and this is one part of boat work I really hate. The ladder has a lot of give, and emphasizes every movement of the boat beneath me as I ascend. Once past the spreaders my legs always begin to shake. It is instinctive. I do wear my sailing harness but never connect it to anything. I think to myself that the trick is not to let go. I reach the top of the mast, and work with one hand while holding on with the other. I cut the old wire free with my knife, and move my unstretched wire dangling from my loosened spinnaker halyard over to the shroud cleat, connecting it with a line through the insulator at the wire's end. This will free up my spinnaker halyard, should I have an occasion to use the spinnaker on the way back.

With nothing else to do I break out the air compressor. This allows me to do a little diving without scuba tanks. The air compressor is mounted on a large

I climb a ladder pulled up by the main halyard.

inner tube, which has a diving flag. One or two forty-foot hoses can be attached, each with a regulator. This will be the first time I use it.

It works fine. I decided to bring this device instead of tanks so that I would not have to look for places to fill air tanks. I test it out first around *Top Cat*, then dinghy it over to a diving mooring. While I have been diving on and off for thirty years I have always used a tank, never a floating air compressor. I have no problems other than getting the big tube and air compressor into and out of the dinghy. I am annoyed a few times when the hose seems to entangle my feet.

. ..reef fish...a huge feather duster...

I go back to the boat for my underwater camera and have a good time trying to take pictures of everything I see -- reef fish, a squid, many corals and sponges, a huge feather duster.   I try to use up all the fuel in the compressor, but fall a little short. The tank holds enough gas to produce air for two people for two hours. I am worn out before the gas tank is empty, even though I waste air as much as I can.

In the afternoon I take yet another trip around the Francis Bay Trail. This time I meet a donkey about halfway up. He passes me by without comment. I see more hummingbirds, and try to take their pictures again. I also try again for a shot of the giant black bees. I see other birds, and I spot a mongoose as I pass the salt pond. The mongoose looks like a long low-slung brown squirrel.

Once again, I encounter a donkey, the same donkey, I think, as before.   I have caught up with him; we are apparently going opposite directions on a circular path. . I also meet up with a photographer on the trail. He has a Nikon with an 800-mm lens and a doubler on a tripod. I take pictures when the opportunity presents itself, but he sits patiently for hours, he says, and waits for one good picture. He tells me of a trip to New Jersey to take a picture of a bird that was sighted 200 miles north of its range — nesting in somebody's backyard.

... I meet a donkey about halfway up.

He used eleven rolls of film taking pictures of this one bird, and waited 18 months before he was able to get a couple of the pictures published. I am impressed. My exertions with the bees and hummingbirds seem trivial compared to his efforts.

Back on *Top Cat* I watch the charter boaters. These boats have the charter company logo all over them. One comes in right behind me. The boaters, consisting of two couples, drop their anchor in 45 feet of water. The anchor goes straight down. They don't back the boat on the anchor, and they absolutely don't dive on it. I suspect they have 100 feet of chain out. Fortunately, it is dead calm tonight, and I will leave in the morning. They go for a swim and start their generator. I think they are having a good time and do not begrudge them their lack of boating know-how. This is a great spot, and I feel kindly toward the charter boaters, as well as the cruisers. I just hope nobody bumps into me in the dead of night.

In the morning I head for Hurricane Harbor on the east end of St. John. It is a very quiet and scenic trip with little wind. The low that has killed the trades will soon dissipate, according to the weather reports, but for right now, there's no wind. I motor the entire way past beautiful lush green hills, granite cliffs, and occasional white sandy beaches. Hurricane Harbor is one of a number of small harbors in Coral Bay. Some of the harbors have mangroves, but not many of them, since the shores of the island are so rocky. Mangroves have a tough time growing in rock.

Much of Coral Bay is over 50 feet deep, not much different from the water outside the bay. The Virgin Islands rise from a bank that is about 100 feet deep, give or take 50 feet. The shallow harbors off Coral Bay are from 10 to 30 feet, a good anchoring depth.

Arriving in Hurricane Harbor, I pass over some water that appears to be sand with some grasses and I anchor. The water is not nearly so clear as the water in Francis Bay. I dive on the anchor and find that while I am anchored in sand, the dark areas are coral communities, not grasses. Coral is not indicated here on the chart, or in the park brochure. I note that when the wind returns to the east my chain could gouge or even topple some of these corals.

I move to a second little anchoring area. The water here is very murky. I cannot see the bottom in 15 feet of water. I put on my dive mask and stick my head in. I see what seems to be sand with some grasses. I drop the anchor, and dive on it. This time it really is sand with grasses. The water is so murky I have to get within a few feet of the bottom to be sure.

Coral Harbor is just outside the park boundary on St. John, and about a mile or so from me, and is said to house the largest cruiser community in the USVI. I motor over to talk to some cruisers and pick up some supplies. Cruisers are not permitted to stay more than 14 days in park waters, a rule no doubt aimed at the live-aboards. Of all the non-park sections of St. John, Coral Harbor is perhaps the most protected from the weather, and hence the logical destination for cruisers.

One cruiser tells me he has been cruising for 13 years but has spent the last four years right here. He says there were few others when he first arrived. He and his wife both work here during peak season (December through April), but they are currently out of work. His wife doesn't mind cruising as long as they stay in harbor, but she would still prefer to live in a house.

I talk briefly with another cruising couple living here who tell me where to go for supplies. Following their directions, I arrive at a dinghy dock next to a marine store. I walk to the deli and buy some sandwich meat, tomatoes, and a kiwi fruit. On the way back to *Top Cat* I note several houses being built in the non-park area of St. John. One is going up right on the beach, just a few feet above the sea. I am astonished at the daring this represents. Florida building codes wouldn't allow it.

Later I stop at Leduck Island. After I land (no easy task since there isn't a beach), I put my small dinghy anchor off the stern and wade in. I tie the painter to a rock on shore. The island is covered with rounded, waterworn rocks. A few birds are on the island, but I see no nests, Then I spot a small sign. I am not supposed to be here. I wade back to the boat, pull up my anchor, and depart.

....spiky black sea urchins...

In the afternoon I take a hike around Hurricane Harbor. I see wild goats, and evidence of many small animals. The shoreline is beautiful. Many small marine creatures, including spiky black sea urchins, cling to the rocks.

Back at the boat I sit listening to the donkeys bray on shore and watching a seagull flirt with me, convinced I will supply some food. If my wife was here she would feed it. It's my opinion that feeding wild birds does them no good. The gull perches briefly on the bow pulpit, then flies around the boat complaining loudly and despairingly about my stinginess. Give up, seagull! I will not feed you! Wait for my wife — she's the soft touch in this family!

In the morning I start a marathon walk around the northeast end of the island. My plan is to start with a section of shoreline and mangroves, then travel a mile or so of open highway, then follow the unmaintained Brown Bay Trail over the hill to the other side, then the unmaintained Johnny Horn Trail to Coral Bay, then return to the boat.

I like long walks, and my wife would never go on this one, so I will do it now. The mangrove part of the walk is not bad, since the mangroves here are sparse, not the dense tangle of roots and branches they tend to be back home in the Keys. The walk over a section of highway 10 is really hard, since the road seemed to go straight up and then down. Virgin Islanders don't have to deal with ice or snow, so in road-building they must feel they can disregard any limits on grade. This is perhaps the steepest road I have ever encountered.

Sections of the Brown Bay Trail are beautiful. From the top of the hill, much of the island chain is visible first to the south, then, farther along, to the north. There is a constant chatter from birds. I meet goats and an occasional donkey in the forest. My nose is assaulted by a bouquet of odors. At times it smells like an herb garden.

The trail is substantial for the first hour, then it peters out and disappears. I head up a dry streambed and eventually find the trail again. It is so dense with thorny brush that the going is very hard. It looks as if the trail is maintained primarily by goat travel and browsing: the brush is cleared for those hikers under a yard tall. Goats become very plentiful in the middle of the island. Their cries often sound to me like human kids calling for their moms. The goats run as I approach, a sign that they are not familiar with the National Park tradition of being fed by friendly visitors.

Eventually the trail comes to the sea on the north side, first to a rocky shoreline, then to a beach. I continue on, alternately losing the trail and regaining it, until finally the trail connects with the Johnny Horn Trail. I take the Johnny Horn Trail back over the hills. At this point in my journey the hills are beginning to feel like mountains. The trail widens, and is much easier to walk.

....overlooking Coral Bay, and I can see Top Cat.

I have now been walking for about four hours and have finished all my water. I am eager to get back to the boat for lunch. The trail branches at several places, and each time I take the branch to the left, since that is the shortest route to the boat.

At long last I find myself at the top of the hills overlooking Coral Bay, and I can see *Top Cat*. I continue on and shortly find the trail-end in a thicket of thorns. It takes me some time to make it from there to the road through the woods. I am glad that this is a small island.

I have a very long lunch to recover my strength and enthusiasm, then pull up the anchor and head for Saltpond Bay. The wind is light, so I motor the few miles to the bay. The National Park Service maintains moorings on three bays on the south of the island, Saltpond Bay, Great Lameshur Bay, and Little Lameshur Bay. All three bays are within a mile or so of each other. I plan to pick up one of the moorings and explore the south side of the island.

When I arrive at Saltpond Bay I see several sailboats and a group of motor-boats anchored there. This is the most popular of the three bays, and has had some boat thievery, according to my guidebook. There is a free mooring, but I decide to try the next bay over. Great Lameshur Bay has only one boat, so I pick up a mooring there.

I dinghy around the bay, looking at the rock beaches, and talk to some cruis-ers. They have been cruising for only two and half years, and have not gone to Venezuela. Their cruising domain is the Caribbean. They have not figured out where to land on the beach, either. There appears to be no easy place to land a dinghy without going over some rocks. The beaches do not look good for walking. The man, like a couple of others I have talked with briefly, wears no clothing, but remains discretely behind a canvas awning as we talk.

Back at the boat I bring out the air compressor, and spend an hour or so surveying the coral in about 20 feet of water, cleaning the barnacles off the boat bottom. A couple of three- or four-foot barracudas follow me for a while as I tour the reef. Then I follow a big stingray. I see no soaring heads, but the area is full of reef fish and corals.

Eventually I return to the boat to work on the bottom. I discover only a mod-est growth on the hull, but I decide to clean it anyway. The job is easiest before the barnacles take hold. I clean the sensor that tells me my speed through the water, as well. For some reason barnacles like to grow on the sensor, and they generally stop it cold. My cleaning complete, I take a shower.

I put up a canvas shade I bought for the boat. It keeps much of the front part of the boat in the shade during the day. Unfortunately, the shade also acts like a giant sail. *Top Cat* moves around if there is much wind. It might help if I moved the canvas further aft, but then it would shade my solar cells.

In the morning I start another long walk. I take the Lameshur Bay trail. This trail is much nicer, and I have no thorny brush to worry about. It is a beautiful walk, and I see many birds, and some good views from the top of the mountains over the southern part of the island.

I dinghy to the other two nearby bays. Little Lameshur Bay has a beach with more sand in it, but still not a beach comparable to those on the north side of St. John. The Saltpond Bay beach is the best, in my view. I take a short walk there to look at the salt pond behind the bay, then snorkel the bay. For perhaps ten minutes I swim through schools of small fish. All the fish in a school are nearly identical in length, ranging from a half-inch to 2 inches. At times two schools merge, then separate to go their own ways. There appear to be no end to these small, almost transparent fish. I am entertained as I glide through school after school of them.

I visit that afternoon for a couple of hours with a longtime cruising couple on their boat. They started cruising at about my age, and have been doing it for 26 years. They spent many of their early years cruising the Bahamas. They say that back then they regularly lived off the sea, picking up lobsters in knee-deep water, and easily catching fish for supper. They say it is much harder now to find either fish or lobsters. When they started there was no GPS, and navigation was always a challenge. The quality of the autopilot and particularly autopilot software has greatly improved, and made long passages much easier. My view is that the next big leap forward for the cruiser will be in communications. We will shortly see the spread of satellite phones as the price for these comes down dramatically in the next decade. The husband is a HAM radio operator, and although the radios are better today, he still communicates with fellow cruisers much as he did years ago. They talk to their circle of cruising friends each morning for an hour on SSB.

Their style of cruising appeals to me. They have always kept a house, and spend a few months there each year through the holiday season and into the new year to complete their taxes. Then they cruise much of the rest of the year. But they do periodically put their boat in storage and do other things for several months at a time. Their cruising time is divided between travel through the Caribbean and stays in a marina in Puerto Rico. While in the marina they plug into shore power and use their boat's air conditioner. They also have TV on their boat, and watch a public broadcasting system channel out of St. Thomas while they are here. They plan to leave for Venezuela soon, since hurricane season is fast approaching, and also because this is their year to have the bottom painted. They had it painted down there three years ago, and only now do they need to do it again. Their 40-foot boat looks comfortable.

In the morning I take a long sail south outside the territorial limit to empty the holding tank, and to enjoy sailing for a while. I take a broad reach out, then a broad reach in toward St. Thomas. It is a dry and pleasant trip in about 15 knot winds out of the southeast.

I anchor in 16 feet of water at Christmas Cove behind Great St. James Island on the southeast corner of St. Thomas. It is bumpy, like so many other Virgin anchorages. The bottom is sand with some grass, so I delay diving on the anchor.

I head out to explore Cas Cay and the lagoon about two miles away across Jersey Bay. First I visit the lagoon. I find the place where old boats go to die in St. Thomas. The canal to the lagoon must contain at least a dozen semi-submerged powerboats. Other old boats are clearly wrecks but somehow are still afloat. Many of these boats may have been wrecked in the last hurricane, Marilyn, in 1995.

Marilyn did considerable damage in both St. John and St. Thomas, but not nearly as much damage as was done by the much stronger Hugo in 1989. This is perhaps the only quiet water around St. Thomas. A sign declares the lagoon itself off limits, but I really do not care to visit anyway. The view across the water was of the town dump. With dead boats and a garbage dump, this area of the island has little to recommend it to visitors, despite the quiet and protected waters here.

Next I visit Cas Cay on the south shore. The west end is protected by an offshore reef and is bordered by mangroves. A sign declares the cay a sanctuary. Another explains the interesting characteristics of mangroves. (By Florida standards this stand of mangroves is insignificant, not worth mentioning.) It is a pretty area, with some white beaches, many shells, and very colorful rocks.

Back at the boat I watch as *Lady Lynsey*, a large catamaran, deposits its huge load of tourists in the water right in front of my boat. They snorkel around for a while, then pile back into the boat and leave. This must be the same *Lady Lynsey* President Clinton and his family were on when they visited the area in January 1997 and snorkeled Lovango Cay.

...Cas Cay... is a pretty area, with...very colorful rocks.

Well, anything Bill can do, I can do, too. (Well, *almost* anything.) It is time to snorkel. The first thing I do in the water is check out the anchor, which I find well dug in. Then I snorkel around the cay in the middle of the anchorage, and then the area the *Lady Lynsey* snorkelers were exploring. The cay was a much better site, but neither site rated with other places I have snorkeled here.

In the morning I pull up the anchor and head out in search of a calmer spot. Christmas Cove is too close to the major traffic lane through Current Hole to be a quiet anchorage, but it is protected from the weather, except perhaps when the wind is out of the southwest. I motorsail with the jib up an hour or so across Pillsbury Sound to St. John, and stop at Hawksnest Bay. I arrive at 10 o'clock. The bay waters are very calm, with several white sand beaches, but no breaking waves, and no swell. I anchor in 15 feet on white sand.

I dinghy back to Cruz Bay for some supplies, a walk, and lunch. I leave the dinghy at the National Park Service's dinghy dock, and take a quick look at their exhibits again. I ask the woman at the desk to play the film. I review the film to see if I have missed anything at the park. I conclude I have seen it all.

I have a West Indies version of chicken and rice in an outdoor restaurant pa-tronized mainly by Islanders. Chickens stroll across my feet looking for scraps as I eat. They have become cannibals, unknowingly scarfing down bits of chicken that have fallen under the table.

This one is convinced I will share my drink.

On my way out I help a motorboat with engine trouble move the short distance over to the dock. Then I circle a large schooner anchored in the sound off Cruz Bay. This is an interesting boat, with a carving of a man instead of a woman on the bowsprit.

I arrive back at the boat in time for an afternoon of continuous rain and take the opportunity to clean up the boat. Later in the evening, while sipping my drink on the back of the boat, I am entertained by another seagull. This one is convinced I will share my drink. It squawks and takes up position in various spots around the boat, usually within a few feet of mine. At one point it sits on the rail about 18 inches from me, precariously balanced, intent on a handout. I give it nothing. Park rules forbid the feeding of animals, I tell my visitor severely, in response to its pitiful and pleading looks.

In the morning, around 9 o'clock, I start out in the dinghy to tour the bay. I am anchored in the southwest corner of the bay, offshore from one of the most exclusive private resorts on the island, the Caneel Bay Plantation, with beach property on Hawksnest Bay as well as on Caneel Bay. The resort, like so much other private property on St. John, is inside the park boundary. The beach is always considered public, and the park service has indicated with green and red buoys the appropriate path in to the shore. There are four such sets of markers in the bay and numerous buoys to mark the exclusion zone for boats. Lounge chairs strew the resort beach, several for each of the dozen or so cottages behind the trees. Many people are out sunbathing, and a few are in the water. I sense I would not be welcome there, so I head for the next beach, which is empty.

The water near the beach appears calm as I approach, but then a large swell arrives and crashes over the back of the dinghy when I reach shore. I jump out and pull the boat up far and fast, then drain the water out. Perhaps I am imagining this, but it seems to me that my arrival at the beach was the exact moment that big swells started to arrive in the bay. I suppose there has to be

...the exact moment when big swells started to arrive in the bay...

some moment when they first arrive. Now I see them crashing one after another on all the bay beaches. Soon the beach I am on seems to disappear as the waves sweep across the entire width. I leave for a bigger beach.

The next beach has four dinghies pulled up on it, and many people. This beach is clearly near the highway, easily accessible. I skip it, and move to the final beach, which is lined with private houses except at the north end. The park has put the red and green buoys at the south end of the beach. I motor in at the appropriate place and try hard to make a graceful entrance. I fail again, with a wave crashing over my stern for the second time this morning. Again I move as fast as I can to get the dinghy well up on the beach and secured.

I set out for the public building at the end of the beach in hope of finding a path to Peace Hill, where the remains of an old sugar mill are located. I pass several people along the way, all very friendly. They talk of the big storm that passed offshore last night that has transformed their normally quiet beach. The beach is indeed very narrow today, and in several places the surf reaches right up to the NO TRESPASSING signs. I manage to get to the north end of the beach, keeping my sneakers relatively dry.

I come across a crew of workers busily cutting back the large seagrape trees, and hacking away vegetation from around the public building, which has no markings. From here I have access to the road. The road is steep, not as steep as the last one I walked, but just as dangerous. There are no shoulders, and the cars really zip by. About half are rental jeeps, the others mostly busses. I reach the parking lot for the Peace Hill ruins in just a few minutes. I have a good view of breakers over Johnson Reef to the north, and of Red Hook across Pillsbury Sound to the south. The guidebooks describe a statue of Christ erected near the ruins, but it is gone. All I can find are bits of masonry that formed its foundation. I head back to the boat for lunch.

I leave in the morning, Saturday, May 16, for Crown Bay Marina. I will prepare the boat for my wife's arrival on the 17th. It is another short trip, about an hour and a half. The only hazard is all the commercial traffic out of Cruz Bay as I depart. I arrive at the marina at 10:30 and have no trouble docking unassisted in the quiet waters at the very long fuel dock. I fill up my tank, and then move to my assigned slip. There are a couple of megayachts here, as well as many smaller sailboats and powerboats.

I discover that a charter boat show is underway at the marina. I wander over to see the charter boats. These are crewed charter boats, and the show is for brokers, not for potential guests. The boats have their amenities on display on deck and around their slips. Most carry scuba equipment. Many carry small boats, including sailboards, kayaks, tubes for towing, and dinghies. Some of the larger boats have a mind-boggling collection of water gear. Menus and nicely appointed dining tables complete with dishes, glasses, and silverware, are displayed. I am hungry just looking at it all.

The facilities at the marina are excellent. I do my laundry and reserve a rental car. I visit the supermarket across the street. The prices are higher than in Puerto Rico, and perhaps twice as expensive as back in Florida.

In the morning I clean the boat one last time. Then I pick up the rental car. Then to the airport, only five minutes from the marina. I meet my wife. She is here! I am no longer a solo cruiser!

I have a good view of breakers over Johnson Reef to the north...

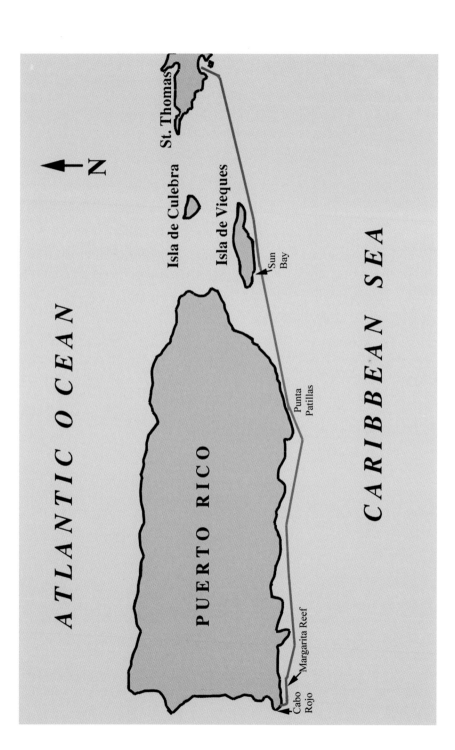

9: Beginning My Return

Later...

Four weeks in the Virgin Islands — it's been wonderful! My wife and I have visited nearly every good anchorage and interesting island we can identify; in the end we feel we have seen the islands. We especially enjoyed visiting Buck Island on St. Croix, the Baths on Virgin Gorda, the Caves at Norman Island, and the endless spectacular beaches of Anegada.

Cruising the Virgin Islands is a special sort of cruising. The people who cruise these waters are mostly charterboaters. They rent a boat and sail it themselves, or they hire a boat with a crew with other people or by themselves, for a week or two. These sailors don't fill the radio waves with nearly so much chatter, they don't use quarantine flags in moving between the British and U.S. Virgins, and they don't anchor nearly so reliably. The waters in the Virgins are generally very deep, with relatively few hazards. The passages are all really short and easy.

All good things must come to an end, and this trip is over for my wife. She's gone back home by air, and now I must follow a longer water route back from St. Thomas, USVI, to Florida, USA. On *Top Cat*, anchored off Water Island, I prepare for my departure. I spend an hour hauling canned goods out of deep storage beneath the two stateroom bunks. I reorganize the boat for the solo trip back.

I am ahead of the game in one respect: my wife brought a few inexpensive parts for my autopilot. I made the necessary repairs the day she arrived, and since then have made a discovery: the autopilot was installed with the wheel and autopilot ring slightly misaligned. This misalignment coupled with my frequent disassembling and reassembling gave the autopilot a tendency to work itself apart. I have remedied the situation by wedging an empty plastic water bottle behind the wheel. Now, though the arrangement may look silly, Otto works perfectly.

...though the arrangement may look silly, Otto works perfectly.

At last I am ready. I weigh anchor and head out into a 15-knot wind past the line of boats anchored along the shore of Water Island. When I first arrived five weeks ago there were many boats anchored here. Now this anchorage is not quite so crowded. Many have headed south with the goal of reaching hurricane-free waters by early July, when the season starts. With the wind off my port beam I feel like I am flying, making well over 7 knots.

This is a wonderful sail, and I feel great. I pass Saba Rock, brilliantly illuminated by the morning sun. I pass fishermen in a colorful boat. I pass Sail

I pass fishermen in a colorful boat.

...like a giant white sail out in the middle of the empty ocean...

Island off the southwest coast of St. Thomas from the east side. I passed this island from the northwest on my way here; it looks the same as from the other side, like a giant white sail out in the middle of an empty ocean.

Incredibly, I find myself on a collision course with another sailboat. How can this be happening yet again, two small boats in this great big ocean, heading directly for each other? I have read that it's been estimated (from collision statistics, I guess) that a collision with another boat will occur once in a thousand long-distance cruises. Yet I have come near colliding with other boats numerous times on this trip alone. Today the wind and seas are moderate, and the visibility good, so I feel no need to make a connection with the sailboat by radio. I have no doubt that the captain of the other boat is thinking the same thing I am — without a course correction, we are in danger of ramming into each other 10 miles from land. While the wind is off my port, it is off his starboard bow, so under international navigation rules I must change course to avoid a collision. Unless he thinks I won't turn in time, he should hold his course. I know this, but I wonder if he knows this; yes, I conclude, he surely does, for he is making no effort to change course. Finally, when I am convinced we really could collide, I turn to starboard and we pass within a couple of boat lengths of each other, smiling and waving.

My immediate destination is Isla de Vieques , with the intent of stopping for the night at Sun Bay on its south coast. This island is larger than St. Thomas, and is mostly uninhabited. I wonder if it has great beaches.

My rate of progress is indeed rapid. No bouncing to windward, no fighting headwinds or current. This is easy sailing, with the wind behind me and a following sea. I reach Isla de Vieques well before noon, with a U.S. Navy destroyer a few miles off my starboard.

The east end of the island is restricted, used by the Navy. There are fine-looking beaches, and I would love to stop. But walking beaches here is not allowed. I chose Sun Bay as my destination for today, since it is on the western end of the island where I am allowed to stop. But I arrive there by 1 o'clock, too soon to quit for the day. I study the situation and conclude that I can make Puerto Rico by sunset. Onward!

Later in the afternoon the wind slows, and the current seems less favorable. I leave the western end of Isla de Vieques, which is almost as empty as the eastern end, and head out for Point Tuna on the southeastern end of Puerto Rico. I realize I must have a motor assist to reach the closest anchorage in Puerto Rico, Puerto Patillas, by sunset.

As before, there are enormous rollers as I approach the southeastern coast, but this time I am traveling downwind. The ocean bottom comes up from a few thousand feet to less than a hundred feet in a tenth of a mile or so, a factor that contributes to the big rollers as a huge amount of moving water tries to fit into a smaller and smaller space.

...there are enormous rollers as I approach the southeastern coast...

I reach the reef off Puerto Patillas about an hour before sunset, and head around it. The reef protects the bay to some degree from weather from the south. My chart warns of rollers in the anchorage, but Van Sant in his book says to move in close for good protection, and he provides directions. I intend to find Van Sant's anchorage.

There are a half dozen jetskiers zipping about, and loud Spanish music everywhere on this late Sunday afternoon. The beach seems to be full of people having a party. Can they do this all night? I hesitate to drop my hook here. Perhaps this will not be such a good anchorage, after all.

Now to avoid hitting a reef Van Sant directs me to head east toward the A-frame house. What A-frame house? I see the beach, I see the ramp, but no A-frame house. I keep moving in, well past the chart's anchorage position. It is getting shallow, now less than 10 feet. I decide to stop. The bottom is grass, and I am holding fine.

I sit with my drink watching the jetskiers scream back and forth, and inspect the shore. I plan no dinghy trips. I have not yet called customs, and if I don't go ashore I won't need to. The wind shifts a little to the south, swinging the boat to the north. Then I see it — the A-frame house, blocked almost entirely from the south by a very large tree! Well, it turns out I am really not far from Van Sant's spot. The anchorage is a little rolly, but not so bad as implied on the chart. I am pleased to observe that the music stops, the party ends, and the people go home. I will sleep tonight.

As I head west in the morning I soon begin to feel large rollers from the southeast, and a strengthening breeze. I move rapidly under full sail, just far enough off the south coast to clear the reefs.

Large stretches of wilderness line the south coast, and much of it is beautiful. I enjoy just sitting and watching the passing scene while sailing. I pass within a couple of miles of Salinas. I wave to the cruisers there, but of course I am too far off shore from them to see me. Near midday I reach Caja de Muertos, one of my favorite spots on my trip down. I pass to its south this time.

Once past Caja de Muertos I have a straight shot to Cabo Rojo on the southwest corner of Puerto Rico, passing south of the Margarita Reef. If all goes well I will park again at Cabo Rojo.

Later in the afternoon the wind begins to pick up, and I pull in my jib. The wind is off my aft quarter, with gusts to 30 knots. Otto has a hard time when the wind blows hard from the stern and there are big rollers. He goes through a period of total incompetence, turning way off track, causing the main to jibe against my preventer, then being unable to regain control. I rescue him. After the third time I decide to take over the steering. It is not hard if you know what to do. The trick, I tell him, is to make large corrections, and to do them fast as that roller comes through. Otto is incapable of learning this simple trick, however, so I stay at the helm and give him a rest.

Then the wind dies. I put up the jib, and Otto goes back to work.
Good, he can do this. I put a music from the 60s CD in my boombox and turn up the sound. I have a good time with my own loud music, far from anybody. I see no boats, neither cruiser nor local. I see no people, just plenty of empty countryside. I move, sing, and shout with the music, feeling totally free to look and act stupid. It is not within my nature to do this sort of thing in public, even after a drink. Without an audience, I really enjoy myself.

Then I look up into the glare of the late afternoon sun and see breakers. For a moment I wonder what those white-topped waves could be, out there off my port side, far away from the land, and then I realize what I am seeing. It is the Margarita Reef! Otto is entirely ignorant of this danger and travels steadily on toward disaster. I grab the wheel and disengage the autopilot, turn the boat sharply to port, head us out to deep water. We pass over the eastern end of the reef, with my depth sensor reporting first 40 feet then 13 feet before settling back to over 20. I see the big breakers now off to my right and realize I could have been there in them. A safe route lies between the outer reef and inner

It is the Margarita Reef!

reefs, but it is narrow. I am prudent, I will not attempt this without some chart study. This small diversion adds to the glory of the afternoon. I sort things out, hand the helm over to Otto, and am soon back moving and singing to the music. I continue down the coast skirting the reef, with my music loud, having a excellent time.

Just before sunset I round the cape, and settle into Cabo Rojo. After my previous stop here, this place seems like home. I love the shallow water and the grassy bottom. There is nobody else around. I anchor in 6 feet of perfectly flat water, have my drink, and call my wife at home. She tells me that she thinks she saw me departing from St. Thomas as she flew over. We compare notes. She remembers a freighter abeam of the catamaran she saw from the plane, and indeed there was one to starboard as I sailed out of the harbor. It may well have been *Top Cat* she spotted. Amazing!

I get up at 5:30 to hear Perfect Paul forecast the weather. Throughout most of the Virgin Islands we had continuous daytime weather reports on VHF. In Puerto Rico I get the VHF weather on the east coast out of San Juan, and also on the west coast out of Mayaguez, though no reception on the south coast. I don't worry about it. The reports from Puerto Rico are mostly in Spanish, but if you wait awhile you will hear an English version. Soon I will be out of range, so I need to practice listening to Perfect Paul on my SSB. The weather report forecasts normal tradewinds.

Just before sunset I...settle into Cabo Rojo.

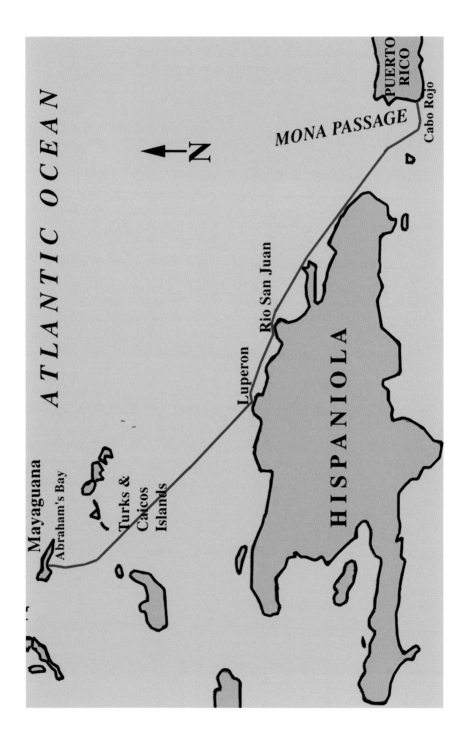

10: The Big Passages

I do not enjoy overnight passages. I like to spend my nights peacefully asleep in my cabin, in a quiet anchorage, not peering anxiously out into the darkness imagining a pod of enraged killer whales or a huge floating container off a container ship lurking along my intended route. However, there are two overnight passages on this trip that can't be avoided. One is the Mona Passage between the Dominican Republic and Puerto Rico. The second is crossing from the Dominican Republic to the Turks and Caicos or to the Bahamas. I also don't have a lot of interest in cruising the waters of the Dominican Republic. My intent is to get this part of the trip over with rapidly, then to travel slowly through the Bahamas, stopping to enjoy a good night's sleep every night.

I leave, heading for the eastern end of Hourglass Shoal in the Mona Passage. Even though it is quiet weather I don't want to pass over the shoal just to save an hour or so of transit time. The winds are light, but I feel no need yet to put on the engine.

A USCG vessel appears off my starboard bow, then crosses ahead of me. I take a picture. The ship turns, and soon is off my port. I think decisions are being made. Will they call, will they board my boat? When the Coast Guard is near I have learned to be sure that the VHF radio is on. Soon I do get a call. What is my last port? What is my next port? My questioner wants some personal data, too. He thanks me and the vessel appears to be leaving.

But five minutes later I see the boat turn and head back toward me. This group is uncertain of how to proceed with me, I think. Soon there is someone on the radio saying a boarding party is on the way. They arrive in a really nice inflatable, and climb up my back steps. One guy stays on the inflatable and circles *Top Cat* while five guys come aboard, all very courteous. The boarding officer asks if I have any guns on board, adding quickly that if I do have one *please* don't pull it out! He seems a bit nervous as he says this. Perhaps an anxious boater has accidentally shot him on a previous boarding mission. I tell him I have no guns. My visitors ask me not about drugs, but about life

A USCG vessel appears off my starboard bow...

preservers. I show them the life preservers, and other safety equipment. They are here, they say, to conduct a spot safety check. I assume that is their alibi, and that they are really here to decide if I am running drugs, or smuggling aliens. They eventually leave, giving me a gold sheet, which means I pass inspection. I have enjoyed their visit, but can't avoid feeling that if I had aliens or drugs aboard, their search was insufficient to reveal either one.

The wind is very light, and I turn on the engine. The boat picks up speed, but with so little wind the jib is useless and the main bounces back and forth with each swell. I lower the sails, disappointed. I hate motoring. A sailboat sails!

About 10 miles out, a bee visits. *I understand,* I tell her (after this much time at sea I am talking to everything, animate or otherwise), *the winds are very light. You are confused. You have not reached land. This is a boat, and we are at sea.* She walks around the helm, and I watch carefully. I advise her of our position. *We are 10 miles from land,* I say. *Better get going if you want to be home by dark.* She takes the advice and flies away. I make my sandwiches.

Then there are more. First ten, then twenty, and soon the boat is full of bees. I put my sandwiches down to look around and bees dive for my food. I find four bees floating in my cup of tea. This is annoying. I am not troubled by a visiting bee or two, but this is a plague. *Who invited you?* I shout. *Get out! Get out now!* They don't leave, so I grab my fly swatter and I spray myself with insect repellent.

I am really annoyed. I jump around and shout and swat. Bees die right and left. Soon there are dozens of dead bees. More are coming all the time. They are slow-moving, and sometimes I kill two or more at each blow. They are all over me, and I am continually shaking them off. Strangely, they don't sting. Perhaps it is my coating of repellent that protects me.

...bees dive for my food.

Bees come and inspect their dead sisters, and I let them fly away with the message: *This is a death ship. Leave now!* And eventually they do.

I count the dead. I have personally killed about a hundred. That is a heavy burden for a person who never, ever kills bees, or almost anything else.

I look behind me and see some threatening storm clouds. I turn on WX-1 for the VHF weather broadcast out of Mayaguez, the big industrial city and Puerto Rican west-coast port of entry. I listen to the report, warning of a severe thunderstorm drifting northwest off the coast. That location is here, at this exact spot in the Mona Passage. The report is for winds over 35 knots! Worse, this storm comes with lightning. I don't want to lose my electronics. According to the report, the storm is moving northwest at 5 to 10 knots.

The view behind me is frightening. A wall of very dark blue clouds covers about 100 degrees of my view aft. There are places where I see the tornado-like funnels of waterspouts. Lightning flickers and thunder booms. My wind is picking up, and my speed is now 7 knots. Can I out-race it? Is there a direction I can go that will enhance my chances of missing this beast?

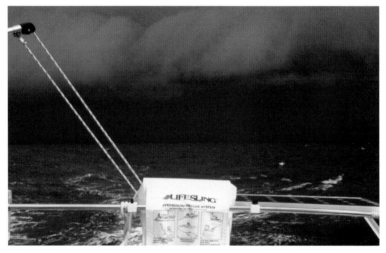

A wall of very dark blue clouds...

I carefully note the borders of the storm relative to my view so that I can judge if it is gaining on me or not. I shift my direction 10 degrees more to the north, and in 30 minutes recheck its size. No change. My wind is about 20 knots, and my speed about 7.

Perhaps this will work out to my advantage. If I can just stay a bit ahead of the storm until it dissipates I will have the best of all worlds, wind and speed, but no rain or lightning. I am prudent, so I pull in my jib, sailing with the main alone. The wind soon grows to 25 knots, not uncomfortable since it is coming from behind me.

After an hour or so the wind picks up some more, and the storm seems to be a little bit closer. The weather report was right on the money. The winds grow to 35 knots, with gusts to 40. I am really moving, over 8 knots with just the main. I slide down some big swells and reach speeds of 10 to12 knots for a moment or two. Exhilarating!

I concentrate totally on steering. Otto is worthless. We have a big swell from behind that comes from a slightly different direction than the wind, and each big wave pushes us left or right. If I don't correct rapidly there is a chance that the wind could overpower the helm and cause us to broach, putting us broadside to the wind and waves. The consequences of a broach in these conditions are not clear (would the boat flip over?), but this is one discovery I don't care to make right now. Or ever, come to think about it.

A light rain begins, and soon has left me drenched. The rain started when the wind picked up. From that point on I am riveted to the helm and have no hope of putting on my rain gear. Obviously I should have expected rain, and could have prepared. Sitting soaked in my bathing suit and T-shirt is not so bad, though, since it's warm out here.

The clouds no longer look so dark. I think the storm is weakening. The wind is definitely easing up. The rain has stopped. I will miss you, big bad storm.

Amazing! Such success! I did keep ahead of the storm until it ran out of steam. My wind diminishes until it is only about 10 knots. I am moving slowly with just the main. The sky is gray everywhere behind me, and the only spots of clear sky lie ahead. I see many large pieces of bamboo drifting by and wonder where they came from.

The view out the stern is very strange. The frothy water there has taken on rainbow colors. What am I seeing? Two patches of frothy water are moving

The frothy water... has taken on rainbow colors.

toward me. Now I understand. Two lines of rainbow are projected on the water and both are pointed at me! The rainbows move closer and closer to me and behind them is a line of rain. Now I can see the rainbow in the sky as well as in the water. I have never seen anything like this before. The rain reaches the boat, without wind. I grab a bar of soap, shuck off my wet bathing suit and T-shirt, and have myself a quick rainwater shower.

A spectacular sunset puts an end to the day.

The rain leaves me and takes away almost all my wind, though I still have big swells. The main makes frightening sail-snapping noises, slamming the boom back and forth with each swell. I will have to pull it down before something tears or breaks. Time to motor. Also time for my evening drink and some loud music to drown out the motor. A spectacular sunset puts an end to the day.

The night comes, and with it utter darkness. I have seen no sailboats since St. Thomas, and there are none tonight, but I do spot two freighters. They are very visible with so many lights. They move much faster than I do, and are headed away from me.

Storm cells swirl around me. When I get close to a storm, my wind picks up. Between storm cells, I have no wind at all. Smaller cells are no problem. My wind rises only to 10 or 15 knots. But there is rain. For a while I turn the usual practice of taking down the sail before the storm upside down — I put the main up if I see what looks a storm, hoping for some accompanying wind. It works! After the storm is gone, my wind dies to a few knots, and the swell drives the main bats. *Fwap-fwap* it goes, swinging from side to side as the boat rises and falls on each swell. Down with the sail again. I complete several cycles of up with the sail, down with the sail. I leave the jib furled. It has been pretty useless tonight, just flapping in the light winds, and flapping harder from side to side in the tailwinds.

Geeps begins to ring. Perhaps he's wet. Uh-oh. Geeps doesn't seem to be changing his position estimate. Hoping to help, I turn him off and restart him. He's refusing to acquire satellites now. Not good. I turn him off, and again I restart. Now he doesn't come on at all. Clearly, there's a problem. What's this? He has a message for me: Receiver failure. This is Geeps's way of admitting that he is not up to the job. I will have to give him the night off and bring out Geeps Junior. Junior is a hand-held battery model and I have no more than about 10 hours of battery supply. I will have to use him to take position fixes now and then, but I will not have the advantage of the continuous display I get with Geeps.

Dawn comes as I reach Cabo Cabron. I have skipped the stop at Samana I took on the way down. I will get there too early in the day, probably around 9 o'clock in the morning, and I won't sleep well at that hour. We are in a brief period of clear weather. The light-colored cliffs of the cape brilliantly reflect the rays of the morning sun. This coastline of the Dominican Republic is uninhabited, and very rugged. There are great green slopes in the background with craggy cliffs dropping abruptly to the sea in the foreground.

The light-colored cliffs of the cape brilliantly reflect the rays of the morning sun.

More rain is on its way. I finally give in and put my rain suit on, both pants and top. I have rain shower after rain shower, and now everything is salt free! Even the bee remains have been washed away. The boat looks clean.

This pattern of weather is not to my liking. We have very light wind, less than 8 knots without the rain. I pull down the sails. Then there is rain, and the wind picks up to 15 knots. I put up the sails. The storm clouds as they approach seem innocuous, nonthreatening, with no thunder or lightning. I don't feel imperiled, but I am very soggy and tired. I continue to sail and motor along the north coast of Hispaniola, with the intent of stopping a couple of hours before sunset. At my present pace I will make Rio San Juan, a small fishing village, at about five tonight.

One more rainstorm is coming, looking gray and diffuse like all the others since the big storm in Mona Passage. I have both sails up, hoping for a 15-knot wind and a good ride. Otto has the helm. *Wow!* In a flash my wind goes from 5 knots to 35 knots! Otto can't handle it! He loses control instantly, sending us broadside into the wind. The boat's strong weather helm just whips us around, pulling the boat out of Otto's control.

I grab the helm and attempt to get us back downwind. We crash through waves, with spray everywhere, as I wrestle with the results of Otto's incompetence. We smash over big swells, dislodging everything on the salon table before I can pull us around. The wind howls through the rigging. Back to sailing downwind we seem fine, but I have to work at keeping us under control with both sails up, unreefed. I feel that if I make a mistake, like responding too slowly to the windward pull from a big swell, we will be in trouble again.

We scream through the water, reaching 10 to 12 knots. It is an exciting ride, and one that keeps me vigilant even though I have been up for 30 hours. This is fun, I think, as long as everything holds together. Downwind is not uncomfortable. There is no spray over the bow, and no slamming of the hull.

Soon the storm is gone, our speed greatly slows, and my tiredness reappears. The sails are up, but now every time I see a storm cell I think about pulling them down. I am probably overreacting. I am very tired.

I pass a really nice looking resort, with a fine white beach and a golf course that goes on forever, perched on high cliffs over the sea. I spot only a few people. Perhaps the cloudy day has kept them away.

Finally I round Cabo Francis Viejo and head to Rio San Juan. My intent is to anchor not far off the swimming beach, following directions in the Van Sant book. This open anchorage is easy to get to. I am so tired I don't want anything tricky. I go to a point well off the beach, and then proceed in to the GPS coordinates Van Sant has supplied. The water is very clear, and it is late afternoon, a time when I can easily see into the water. But I find only beautiful coral on the bottom, and very little sand. Clearly I can't anchor here! This place is too nice for my anchor.

I decide to attempt to anchor next to four old fishing boats near the village, again following the directions in Van Sant. To do this I must follow a route that takes me through a cut in the reef. I head toward what I think is the river at the appropriate heading, then cut in toward what I think is the boatyard. I go very slowly with my sails down, and both engines turned on to give me extra maneuverability. There are supposed to be reefs to the left and to the right, but it is calm, and I see no waves breaking. It is also getting darker, and I can see the bottom much less clearly now. I have no chart that gives me bottom depths, just the sketch chart from the guide. My depth readings show less water than the estimates in the guide. I wonder if I am on the right track. Is that float the float referred to in the guide? I could buy a better float than that one at Kmart for a few dollars. I keep moving, never in water under 8 feet deep, and soon I am in opaque water, muddy water over a muddy bottom.

This is the mouth of the Rio San Juan, a small river, but I am thankful for it. I join four old fishing boats. What a group!— four old fishing boats, and one rather expensive catamaran sailboat. My boat is fiberglass, and full of elec-

I join four old fishing boats.

tronics. My neighbors are wooden, and look very used. I definitely don't fit in. I wonder if they have many visitors? Soon a small motorboat filled with kids comes by. Everyone waves.

As I sit in my deck chair having my drink and looking at the sunset I wonder if it was skill that got me through the reef. Since there are no detailed charts of the waters here, perhaps the trip in is easier than I thought. Van Sant indicates reefs, but how shallow are they? Maybe I was way off the track and just passed over the reef. Or maybe I was just lucky. In any case I must get out in the morning. Whatever it was that got me in I hope will get me out again safely.

I am exhausted and have a good sleep, but get up at 5:30 for the morning weather report. The weather sounds like it will be fine. I head out, carefully retracing my path in. All four fishing boats are still here. I also see a new boat, a real yacht, much larger and nicer than *Top Cat,* out in the bay a few miles from me. He can't be anchored. It is over 100 feet deep at his location! I head out toward him. He is drifting, and calls to ask me about the way in. I tell him to look for the float, and he heads into the unknown in his very expensive yacht, depending on the advice of a stranger. I look back as I depart. And yes, following my directions, he does indeed make it through.

The wind is light, and I motorsail to Luperon. I adjust the engine speed for an arrival at four or five. There are storm cells today, as yesterday, but they are significantly fewer. I continue to see many rainbows, including a perfectly

I continue to see many rainbows...

complete double rainbow arch. I don't recall seeing one so perfect on the open water ever before. I see many rainbows high in the sky on clouds. This is certainly a great place for rainbows as well as rain. But there is relatively little wind and I proceed with both sails up and a motor assist.

In the afternoon the wind dies completely for a while, then picks up late as I approach Luperon. Finally, within 10 nautical miles of Luperon I am able to cut the engine assist and proceed under sail alone. Since I have been through the Luperon channel once, I feel confident I can do it a second time. It is fairly rough when I arrive directly north of the entrance, yet I do not see the break-

...fishermen in a little boat...

ers on the north side of the channel. I see the breakers on the south side, I see fishermen in a little boat and — amazingly — also a new red float that marks the south side of the channel! Progress has been made since my last visit many weeks ago! I pull in the jib, drop the mainsail, and head in with both engines on for extra maneuverability. I stay in deep water until I am inside the marked channel, apparently hitting the center of the channel better than I did last time.

As I reach the inside harbor I am surprised by the large number of cruisers anchored here. Not as many as in April, but still a couple of dozen. I assume most of these boats are on the way south to Venezuela for the hurricane season, although I suppose some may stay right in Luperon. Luperon is not my idea of a tropical paradise.

I arrive at about 4 o'clock in the afternoon with my yellow quarantine flag flying, expecting the immigration and customs officials. I see them in their small boat checking other boats in the harbor, and wave. I believe they see me, and I await their arrival. They do request that boaters do not go to them. If they come, I will order some gas.

I filled up on gas at Crown Bay Marina in St. Thomas, topping off my main tank and filling four plastic gas containers. I have used about half this gas, which has supplied about 60 hours of motoring on one engine at two-thirds speed. I have measured my fuel consumption rate many times since the only useful measure for fuel is engine hours. The range over the water relates to speed, and my speed over water is totally a function of the wind and wave conditions. My surface speed is also a function of current. One engine at two-thirds power going into a 20-knot headwind will make only a knot or two of progress, depending on the waves. But with no wind and little sea the speed will be about 5.5 knots, clearly a very big difference. I used 30 hours of gas during all the windless periods crossing the Mona Passage and the north coast of Hispaniola, but the 30 hours I have left is probably enough to get me to George Town with some reserve. In the worst case I may just have to wait for windier conditions. I resolve not to go ashore, and to leave without checking through customs and immigration if they don't show up tonight.

At 5 o'clock I see the motor boat carrying the officials head to the dock, and I see no more of them. I asked the *Commandante* last time what his hours were. He told me they worked 24 hours a day!

I weigh anchor at 6:15 in the morning after the weather report from Perfect Paul, and head toward the mooring on West Caicos. If my progress is slow I plan to stop at a mooring, or anchor off the West Caicos beach, otherwise I plan to proceed to Mayaguana.

Out in the open ocean I discover that the weather report is promising, with 10- to 15-knot winds from the southeast, and moderate seas. The boat motion is nasty, very rolly, since I am almost in a dead run, and big swells continually push me through 50-degree swings. Somehow Otto is able to keep control. I settle in with a book.

We pass a tug pulling a barge very similar to the one I saw here coming down. And later I see a sundog, a halo around the sun, directly overhead. The sky has very high cirrus clouds. I see no rain clouds.

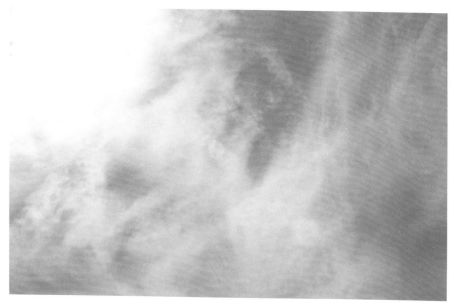

...a sundog, a halo around the sun.

Later in the day I begin to see them everywhere.

In the afternoon I begin to wonder about the weather report as the wind picks up, and storms appear everywhere. Gusts regularly reach 22 or 23 knots. The boat is very difficult to move around in because of the motion caused by going almost directly downwind.

I have my evening drink and dinner and settle down for a long night. I have made good progress and expect to be at West Caicos very early. If it is early enough to allow an afternoon arrival at Mayaguana I will not stop.

It is a dark and spooky night. I have my running lights on, but no others so that I can see what little there is to see. There are clouds everywhere around the horizon, and everywhere there is the flicker of lightning. I glimpse a few stars here and there, but most of the sky is covered with clouds. Until there is a flash of lightning, I see almost nothing. Then everything is momentarily illuminated, and I can see strange cloud shapes everywhere.

We continue under Otto's control, and for a while I sit in the salon, plotting our course. I turn on the overhead light only briefly to check the charts; I need my night vision. It is rough out here. I have the entire boat closed up except for the door between the salon and the cockpit. While there is no continuous spray, each time a big swell hits us we swing into the wind and sometimes hit a bit wave that splashes over the sides or on the front windows. I turn off the light and emerge from the salon to check on Otto, and raise my head just six inches above the salon top.

WHAMP! I am hit on the left side of my face by something.

The something has significant weight, and my face hurts. It seems to me that the blow was accompanied by the flutter of wings. It is totally dark, and hav-

...under the salon table...a flying fish.

ing just turned off the light my eyes are not yet adjusted to the dark. I can see almost nothing. I am flustered and shocked. I wonder if the thing is still here, and fear creeps in. Is it a great terrible beast, or only a seagull? I am inclined to believe it's a terrible beast. Then I begin to smell fish. I grab the flashlight and look all around. Finally I locate it, under the salon table. Not a monster or a seagull, but a flying fish.

I carefully scoop him into a bucket...

This is not a dangerous beast. In fact, it is a very pretty translucent blue fish, about 6 inches long, with great diaphanous wings, like dragonfly wings, only much, much bigger. I feel instantly sympathetic for the fish since he is probably even more stunned than I am. I carefully scoop him into a bucket, and toss him overboard. I hope he recovers. He is obviously a flying fish athlete, capable of leaping large boats.

I see lightning and hear thunder from directly ahead. Still flustered from the flying fish episode, I pull in the jib and take down the main. I motor directly into the storm, and soon have over 30 knots of wind and very heavy rain. The wind shifts to the southwest. My visibility is close to zero.

The rains die, but the winds remain at 20 out of the southwest. Whatever happened to the consistent tradewind I should get here? I put up the main with a single reef, and unfurl the jib.

In an hour the wind dies completely, and I put on the motor.   There are still storms everywhere, and I expect some wind soon. But for hours I get no wind, just rain showers.

Then the wind really picks up, and I pull in the jib. Then it dies, I see storms, and I drop the main. Throughout the night I keep busy putting the sails up and taking them down as the wind and rain comes and goes.

I am thankful for morning, for at least now I can see. We are well past West Caicos, and heading for Mayaguana. But the day continues much as the night, with the winds coming and going, and with the storms coming and going. When the wind is on, it is strong, and we make great progress, usually over 7 knots.   When it is dead, I turn on the engine, and our progress is nearer 5 knots.

After lunch the winds shift to the northeast, and I tack to windward to Mayaguana. The weather has been strange for this trip, very strange.

Finally, as I near exhaustion, we reach Mayaguana. My original intent was to park off the west end, at Betsy Bay, in an open water anchorage in the lee of the island. But now I wonder about the weather. What is the lee of the island? Will I see winds tonight out of the southwest and northeast, as I have today? With a southwest wind I will be exposed in Betsy Bay. I decide to enter Abraham's Bay, even though the winds appear to have shifted back to the south-east.

I drop the main and furl the jib outside the west entrance, and proceed very carefully with both engines. I sit on top of the hardtop, and watch the water. I planned my arrival to have the sun high over the back of the boat to aid in seeing coral heads. This time I follow the chart, and check my depth readings against the charted positions very carefully. I have no trouble entering, but am now more than ever convinced that the charted depths are not quite right. I see 8-foot depths where the chart has 12, and I see heads where the chart has none. It is an easy entrance, though, since the sun is high and I see all the dangers very clearly.   Once inside I spot more heads, and I guide *Top Cat* carefully around them. This is no time for Otto to be in charge. I let him rest. Soon I am in, and head for a patch of clear white sand to anchor. I select one not far from some big heads in 18 feet of water, but well clear of coral.

Once anchored, I head out in the dinghy to dive the big heads. I put out my dinghy anchor and slip over the side into the water to explore the nearest head. It is a little coral city. It rises 10 feet or so up from the sandy bottom and features a wide variety of corals. There are many star and pillar corals. There are sea fans and sponges. And there are fish everywhere. The entire city is about 15 feet wide and 30 feet long. It rises to within four feet of the surface. I get back into the dinghy and go to another head. This one is even bigger, and rises to about 3 feet from the surface. *Top Cat* could hit this one. I move on to a third, smaller head, perhaps five feet from the surface.

Later, sitting on the deck with my drink, I reflect on the weather I have seen in this 200-mile passage. I left Luperon with settled weather. We had 10 to 15 knot winds out of the east to southeast for several days, and these conditions were predicted for the foreseeable future. These wind strengths are consistent with the prevailing conditions, as indicated on my pilot chart for June.

But I missed the significance of one other element in the weather report, "widely scattered showers and thunderstorms." As it turned out, I spent most of my last 33-hour trip under the influence of one storm or another. I had periods of no wind, and winds over 30 knots. I had a few hours of wind out of the southwest, and a few hours of wind out of the northeast. My conclusion is that "widely scattered showers and thunderstorms" means a range of wind conditions.

I am now finished with the long passages, and plan to stop at the end of each day's sail to anchor and get a good night's sleep.

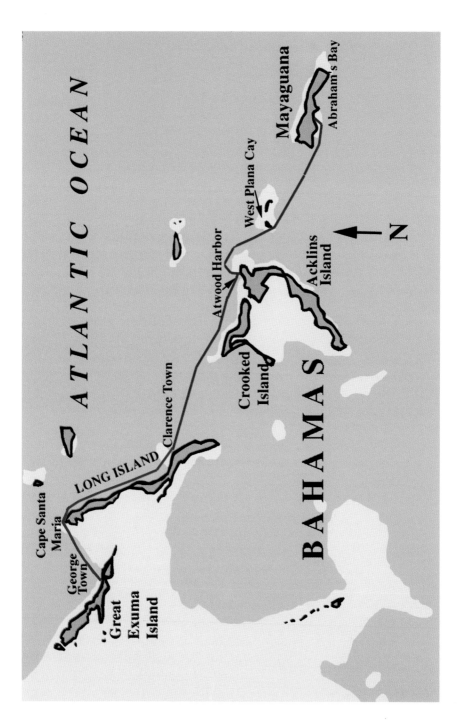

11: Sliced!

I wait until 9 o'clock to depart out the west entrance of Abraham's Bay, which ensures that I have sufficient light from behind me to see the heads. Once in open water I turn the boat into the wind and put up the main, and then pull out the jib. I see a large sailboat approaching, the first sailboat I have seen since Luperon. As I sail off, I see that the boat pauses for a while at the entrance to the bay, then heads off in the direction I am going. They were clearly considering going in, but in the end decided not to try. A good choice, since they would have been traveling into the sun. I think that they should head around to Betsy Bay at the west end of the island where the dangers from heads are less, and that's what they do.

After a brief interval of morning sunshine, the clouds begin to march across the sky. But these are high-flying cumulus clouds, and I don't expect much bad weather from them.

A second boat comes by, a large sportfisherman, bouncing into the wind and sea. This kind of powerboat has a raised foredeck, a flared bow, and a flying bridge over a large cockpit. Perhaps it is headed for a fishing trip to Mayaguana. It produces an incredible amount of spray as it parts the water. For those aboard it is a noisy, bouncy, but extremely rapid journey.

...a large sportfisherman, bouncing into the wind and sea.

I have a short 35-mile trip to West Plana, and I am there about 4 o'clock. As I arrive I see a second sportfisherman head out past me, splashing through the water, and a sailboat appears, lingering off the south coast of West Plana. Later, the sailboat retreats back to the sheltered water in the lee of the island. As I round the south coast of the island my wind picks up to 22 knots, and the bottom appears very clearly in 60 feet of water. I round up in a beam reach hitting 9 knots in the final moments of the day's sail — I am really flying!

The sailboat has anchored ahead of me off the beach, not far from my intended anchorage. As I reach a point just south of my destination I pull up into the wind and drop the sail. I motor in with the sun over my back watching for heads, and anchor in 12 feet of water over sand, about a quarter of a mile from the other sailboat.

I hop into the water in snorkel gear to check the anchor and the heads. The anchor is well buried in deep sand so I continue on to explore the bottom. The first head community I visit is full of sea fans of all colors, and some pillar coral, and barrel sponges. It rises about 4 feet from the sandy bottom and leaves plenty of room for boats above it. There are lots of crevices for lobsters here, but I see none. I do see a grouper, and think of a good fish dinner. I visit several heads out in the deeper water west of the boat, all very much alike. Then I head toward shore. On the way I pass many smaller coral communities and many rocky shelves. I keep looking for lobsters, but find none. I also pass a large sandy area in about six feet of water. I regret that I didn't move the boat closer to shore. I swim right up, passing over a rocky shelf in a foot of water right next to the beach. I leave my mask and flippers, and head out down the beach for a run, the first run since I ran back to the boat when I left my wife at the airport in St. Thomas.

The sand is very soft. I keep moving from the surf to higher up the beach and back looking for firm footing. Occasionally I have firm sand, but mostly my run is over soft and fluffy sand at the start. I run to the south shore mostly along the surf line. The waves begin to come in diagonally; they have created a 2-foot ridge of sand at the water line. Here the sand is a little firmer. My run improves. The south coast ends at a natural jetty. Beyond there is the east coast, and very rough water. The change is enormous, with pounding surf and opaque water. The east coast beach is covered with flotsam and jetsam. I run back to my snorkeling gear, a little tired from my exertions. I rest for a moment, admiring this beautiful beach, which becomes rocky farther to the north. I slide into the water, and over the rocky ledge toward deeper water.

With my facemask no more than 8 inches off the ledge I startle a small flounder lying motionless, completely camouflaged. It glides away. This small fish, with both eyes on one side and colored perfectly to match the rocks, is an expert at moving through the water with body plane horizontal, eyes looking up. I follow it for a few seconds, then continue on back to the boat.

In the boat I have my drink, listen to the BBC, and think about the next leg of my trip. My snorkeling has convinced me that I can leave early, without fear of heads.

I leave at 6:30 in the morning, intent on arriving early at Landrail Point on the west coast of Crooked Island. It is a windy morning, with 20 knots of southeast wind and some rollers. I put up the main so that I don't have to do it in the rougher seas farther off the island. There is a strong pull on the anchor, so I put both engines on slow forward, and move to the front to pull in the anchor. Once the anchor clears the bottom I move fast to secure it in time to rush back and halt our rapid movement toward the shore.

Unfortunately, a big roller causes me to lose my balance and I fall onto the side of the anchor locker. I am greatly annoyed — it hurts enough for me to

...I fall into the side of the anchor locker.

know I have another cut to bandage, one that could keep me out of the water for a few days.

I finish securing the anchor and run back to the helm, and turn the boat quickly seaward. We are never in less than 10 feet of water. As I slow the engine, I glance over at the controls and notice that there is blood everywhere. I look down into the cockpit and it is full of blood. There is a trail of blood leading out to the anchor locker. I have no doubt about whose blood this is.

I grab some paper towels and try to stop the flow from my left arm. It takes me a minute to summon the nerve to look at what I have done to myself. I have a gaping cut that seems to be several inches long. While my skin tends to cut easily, I am utterly amazed that I have done so much damage to myself. I see what appears to be bone for the entire length of the cut, but that can't be, I think. It does look white in there except for the blood. But my hand and arm still function, so there is obviously no muscle or nerve damage.

After I have the boat on a steady course I break out the medical kit and bandage the wound. I have to use three separate bandage squares because I have nothing large enough to cover it. Since the cut is on the back side of my left arm there is no way I could stitch this thing, even if I had the tools, capability, or fortitude. I can just barely bend my arm enough to see it. Still, it will need some stitches if it is to heal. What am I to do?

I have not yet cleared customs and immigration into the Bahamas. I do not worry about this now. It is permissible to anchor in Bahamian waters on the way to a port of entry. My intention is to clear in at George Town, since there is no other port of entry on my route. Until I clear I should not go ashore, or procure Bahamian services. I am sure there is an exception to this in a case of medical need. I definitely have a medical need.

I head for Atwood Harbor on Acklins Island, about 15 miles away. Landrail Point is another 20 miles or four hours beyond Acklins, and I know that it is important to get the stitches in soon. Besides, it is not clear that I would make the Landrail Point anchorage in time to find medical care in normal business hours. But I know that there is no settlement near Atwood Harbor: I will need ground transportation, probably to Spring Point, twenty or so miles south. Chester, the closest settlement, is two miles away. I know that Landrail Point has its own clinic. Landrail Point will be my backup.

As I approach the Acklins I call on VHF channel 16 for assistance from any local resident. I repeat the call several times with no answer. There is no chatter on Channel 16. I then include the term medical assistance in my message, and soon get a reply from a man on Crooked Island, some 20 miles west. I ask him to apprise the Spring Point clinic on Acklins, the one my guidebook says has a doctor, of my need for stitches and to have them call me on channel 16. I tell him that I plan to go to Chester to find ground transportation to Spring Point. I ask him to call me back if he discovers this is not a viable plan.

Atwood Harbor on the northeast coast of Acklins Island is very easy to enter. The cut between the reefs is broad and simple to find. The harbor is beautiful, very well protected except from north winds. Several other boats are already there when I arrive, two sailboats and a flush-deck powerboat cruiser, perhaps

...Atwood Harbor on Acklins Island...

45 feet in length. This is my kind of harbor, I think, as I pull up to the southeast shore in sand with about 8 feet of water. I drop the anchor and settle in a few hundred feet from the other boats.

I talk to my sailboat neighbor in front of me, asking him what he knows about the clinic. He is a single-hander like me, traveling in company with the other sailboat. Both are trying to make it to Venezuela. "Late in the season, aren't you?" I ask. (It's now late June.) He says there are plenty of hurricane holes in the Dominican Republic. He tells me that the skipper of the large powerboat knows about the clinics, and that he has been to Chester and knows the way.

It is 11:30. I have a quick sandwich for lunch and head over to the powerboat. I find the skipper on the deck and ask him how to get to Chester. I tell him I need to find a clinic to put a few stitches in my arm. He tells me he knows somebody in Chester who can tell me where to go. He calls the man on the radio. Then he comes back and tells me that somebody has already been sent to get me. He says "Look over there, that may be him now."

I look to the west shore, about a mile away, and see a figure on the shore. I head out in my dinghy at top speed. I land on the beach, and sure enough the man is waiting for me! He is there to provide me transportation to the clinic. He is a big black man in a one-piece blue coverall. He wears gold-colored metal pins with numbers on both shoulders, and so he looks rather official. I ask him how long the trip is to the clinic, how much it will cost. "Don't worry about that," he says. Apparently, transportation is funded by the government under certain circumstances.

We travel for miles over rocky sand roads south through Acklins. The coun-

...over rocky sand roads south through Acklins.

tryside reminds me of the Florida Keys, with low scrub and coral rock. My driver has a Ford Explorer. I wonder how the suspension system survives. This is the place to have an extended warranty!

We pick up another man waiting on his front porch along the way, and drop him off at a restaurant. Half the houses I see seem to be boarded up, empty. My driver says the residents have gone off to Nassau. He says there are 500 or so people in the Acklins, scattered among a dozen or so little villages. Tourism is the main business, I think, but I see no tourists. He says the tourists come here for the fishing.

Eventually we get to the clinic. The driver says he will wait and take me back when I am done. Two Bahamian nurses greet me, one near my age and one in her twenties. They lead me into a room with a desk and piles of boxes. I sit down on the plastic chair at the desk. They have packed up their equipment at this clinic, which they call the Mason Bay clinic, and at the clinic in Spring Point, about 9 miles down the road, so that the two buildings can be renovated. (They themselves work for the clinic in Spring Point.)

...the Mason Bay clinic...

The two nurses examine my wound and wrinkle up their faces as if to say, "Oh-oh. This doesn't look so good." The older woman, the one who seems to be in charge, says she will stitch it up for me. She begins to rummage through the boxes and bags looking for things. Every once in a while she finds something and tosses it on the desk. The younger woman, who reminds me of a young Dionne Warwick, sits outside the doorway where there is a good breeze, but leaps up every once in a while to help look for something. After about a half-hour the younger woman goes off with my driver. They return with another middle-aged woman who introduces herself as the resident nurse at the Mason Bay clinic. She consults with my nurse.

After a half-hour of more searching it is clear they can't find what they need. The Mason Bay nurse suggests they go to Spring Point to pick it up. But then it is discovered that nobody has the key to the Spring Point clinic. I have been there about an hour and a half, and feel fortunate that they have no other patients. I ask them about other patients and they say they don't usually have many. At last they decide to make do with the supplies they have been able to find, and begin to work on my wound. My nurse says the cut is 4 1/2 inches long, and sews up the wound with 19 stitches, then puts a bandage on it that goes all the way around my arm. She says I must have the bandage changed in 3 days and the stitches removed in 5 to 7 days. She gives me penicillin pills. Here, it appears, the nurse does everything, including dispensing the medicines. She also collects money. She tells me they are now required to collect money under a new government policy. She collects $37. I have the feeling they did a good job. The nurses have all been very nice, and I thank them profusely.

My driver takes me back to Atwood Harbour. He says there is no charge for his service, but that I am free to give him something. I give him a $30 tip. I feel relieved to have this ordeal behind me and resolve to move around the boat with greater care.

I explore the beaches around Atwood Harbour for a while, then dinghy back to the boat. The beaches are beautiful, and empty. There are two small cable houses (which contain equipment for underwater cables — possibly telephone cables) just off the beach at the north end of the harbor, but no residences.

I leave in the morning for Clarence Town, on Long Island. This is a long trip, but from the chart it looks like an easy harbor to enter, and I think I can make it before dark. It is very quiet when I leave, and I have no trouble pulling up the anchor with one arm. I am reluctant to do much with my left arm for fear of pulling out the stitches, something the nurses warned me about. There is so little wind that I begin the trip with both sails and a motor assist.

Along the way I decide to use the small windlass to help me pull up the anchor at Clarence Town. While it is calm I crawl out on the port bow to work on the anchor chain. I remove the 40 feet of 5/16-inch chain and put in its place a doubled-over 7-foot length of 5/16-inch chain. This gives me only 3 1/2 feet of chain, which should allow the windlass to pull the anchor nearly completely out of the water. Of course, I will lose holding power, since the pull on the anchor will have a larger vertical component. It is the chain coupled with a long rode that assures that the pull on the anchor is mostly horizontal along the bottom.

The weather report promised 15- to 20-knot winds out of the southeast, but we have much less wind. The wind is directly from behind at under 10 knots. I run for a while without the engine, but progress is slow. I construct a table, as I usually do, of the range to our destination, bearing (direction to the new anchorage), and the average needed speed to complete the trip two hours before sunset. As the day progresses my needed speed to complete the trip increases from 5 knots to 6 knots, and even a little higher. Once over 6 knots I know I must turn on the engine.

I motor with both sails up for most of the rest of the day and arrive at Clarence Town at about 6 o'clock. There are few hazards here. Reefs lie on both sides as I enter the harbor, but the opening is very large. Several boats are anchored near the town when I arrive. Since I will not be going to town, I see no advantage in anchoring near them.

I anchor in sand a mile or so away across the bay in about 8 feet of water, using the windlass to drop the anchor. I have to go to the bow first to release the anchor, and to open the anchor locker. Then I have to go back to the helm to lower the anchor. I get the anchor down, and set it well. There is nothing here but sand. I feel secure.

I watch the sunset over the town with my evening drink. The town is very picturesque, dominated by two large and handsome churches. I resolve to walk around the town on my next trip here.

I... arrive at Clarence Town...

After a quiet night I weigh anchor around 7 o'clock. I test the windlass system. I remove the bridle and motor toward the anchor, engaging the windlass to pull in the rode. I have no problem pulling the anchor almost completely up. I can see it just below the bow. However, when I release the windlass switch to move to the front of the boat to secure the anchor, the weight of the anchor causes the windlass to slip the rode back out. So I arrive at the front with the anchor at the bottom again. Clearly, the windlass has been damaged. I know that my most recent use of the windlass has been with my wife's assistance. With one person at the helm and another at the bow, the windlass operation goes well. I decide to put my 40 feet of chain back on and forget the windlass. Though it is heavy, I like the security of my big anchor and lots of chain.

The wind is very light again today as I head out toward the north end of Long Island. Again, I start with both sail and motor. After a few hours I turn the engine off, but travel is very slow. My destination tonight is Calabash Bay. I would like to be there well before sunset so I can explore the nearby lagoon.

The wind is light all day. I motor for about 7 hours. It is so calm that I park on the west side of Cape Santa Maria instead of in Calabash Bay. This will allow me to leave early in the morning without worrying about the poor visibility when I exit the reef surrounding the bay.

...a very pretty area, with white sand beaches...

...and limestone caves...

I spend a couple of hours exploring the Cape Santa Maria area and lagoon in the dinghy. This is a very pretty area with white sand beaches and limestone caves.

I pass a group of people from a luxurious catamaran powerboat who are snorkeling from their tender off the beach. Their tender is several times a large as my dinghy. It is hoisted by crane onto their foredeck while underway. I dinghy into the bay, and into the lagoon on the north end of the bay.

The Cape Santa Maria Club is located on the south side of the lagoon, where many small boats are moored. A swift current surges through the entrance. I pass over a large ray as I motor in. The water has a range of depths here. In some places, just a few inches of water covers white sand; in others there's a couple of feet of water over turtle grass; in still others, the water is more than 10 feet deep. I motor through the deeper water and around the edge where I can, always trying to avoid harming the living world of the shallows.

On the north side of the lagoon I discover three limestone caves. It is a very peaceful place without another soul around. Seabirds dot the land, sea, and sky. I hear the sounds of birds coming from the land, but cannot see them. I

...the remains of a lobster dinner.

see nobody at the Cape Santa Maria Club, either. Eventually I leave and drive awhile through the bay. The water is so clear that I can watch the fish around the corals as I pass. On one patch of rock I spot the remains of a lobster dinner.

I return to *Top Cat* in time for the 6 o'clock Perfect Paul weather report and I mix my evening drink. The weather is dominated by a high to our north that doesn't seem to want to move. It brings weak winds below the high, and southwest winds above it. If the high doesn't move for a week I will be battling a headwind crossing the Gulf Stream and traveling west along the Keys!

I weigh anchor and head out at 6 in the morning for George Town. It is totally quiet. I have no trouble retrieving the anchor using my good arm for the heavy pulling.

Not a ripple stirs the water. The bottom is so easy to see it seems as if the water has vanished under me. I head out under power alone, with Otto at the helm. I stand at the bow and study the bottom as we pass. First there is only sand, then coral and fish, then the bottom slopes down quickly. I follow it until the depths exceed a hundred feet or so. Soon the water is thousands of feet deep.

I calculate that I will arrive in George Town later in the morning with a couple of hours of fuel left. I do seem to be cutting it a little close considering I started from St. Thomas with 60 hours of fuel. I could have waited for better weather, but the wait might have been days or weeks. The long-term forecast, looking out five days, projects no change. In fact, for each day since I left Cabo Rojo in Puerto Rico the outlook portion of the weather report has projected no change in weather conditions. This does not encourage one to wait for better weather, unless of course, one has nothing better to do.

I am sure I could have used less fuel in getting here, but not much less. It is important to arrive at each anchorage in daylight. To do this I need the engine to keep up my speed in light winds. In some cases I could have taken smaller steps, or arrived at the anchorage later and saved fuel. I probably could have traded two days and a few daylight hours for an extra 10 hours of fuel.

I arrive on schedule off Fowl Cay at about 10 o'clock, with good light. The Fowl Cay entrance into Elizabeth Harbour is not illustrated on my chart, or in the Bahamas cruising guides, but it is suggested by Van Sant. The route has the advantage of not being into the morning or afternoon sun no matter what the time of day. Further, it is very simple. The route does a half circle about Fowl Cay, always giving the helmsman something nearby to look at. I like the route. I am soon in Elizabeth Harbour.

The trip from here to George Town is easy since it is direct to a couple of stakes and then past a barrel. After that there are no hazards of note. A good deal of the bottom between Stocking Island and Great Exuma Island was dredged by the United States during WWII to allow seaplanes to land. The water is all about 8 feet deep with a featureless sand bottom.

...and then past a barrel.

...a ferry is...towing somebody's sailboat.

I pass a group of three powerboat cruisers anchored off Stocking Island. This seems to be about as far south as the powerboaters go.

This is such a big harbor, and there are so many pretty little beaches and coves, that I can understand why cruisers spend so much time here. One could spend months just exploring the islands around George Town. However, right now, there appear to be few cruisers anchored off Stocking Island, far fewer than in April. I watch the boats; a ferry is hauling not only people and their cars and trucks, but is also towing somebody's sailboat.

I head around to Regatta Point and anchor near where I stopped on the way down. Only a dozen or so boats are here today. I have lots of room. I put down my anchor and 40 feet of chain, and another 10 feet of rope in 8 feet of water. I'm not going anywhere.

I leave instantly in the dinghy to check in and find the clinic so I can have my wound looked after. It is now 11, and I recall that the clinic closes for the day at 1 o'clock. I dinghy to the dinghy dock behind the Exuma Markets on Lake Victoria. It is my second time through, and I know my way around pretty well. It takes me only 15 minutes to clear customs and immigration. Unlike in the Dominican Republic, there are no requests for tips here to clear in, and there is no waiting for the customs and immigration personnel to visit your boat.

The clinic in George Town is much fancier than the one I visited on Acklins. Here they have a receptionist. I tell her that I would like to get the dressing on my wound changed. She ushers me in immediately to see the nurse. The nurse here looks much more official than the ones on Acklins: she is wearing a white uniform, right down to white shoes and stockings. She cleans the

wound and applies a new bandage. She, too, is kind and professional. I tell her
that I expect to be in Nassau when the stitches are to be removed. She tells me
where to go to have the stitches removed there, and gives me a little card to
present explaining what I need. I pay $2 for the service at the receptionist. I
pass the doctor on the way out and say hello. My recuperation seems to be
going very well indeed, and medical care has not been expensive. I resolve to
have all my future injuries in the Bahamas.

I stop next at the market to buy some groceries and take them all back to the
boat. Food here is not cheap, but the store is well-stocked and has just about
everything I need. After lunch I pick up fuel by dinghy, making two trips with
my 6-gallon plastic containers, and have two of my three small propane bottles
filled. I buy the first load of gas on credit, paying $2.85 per gallon, and the
second load with cash at $2.71 per gallon.

I pass several cruisers, and we chat. By late afternoon just about everybody
seems to be asking me about my accident and the 19 stitches. News spreads
quickly here.

I try several times during the day to get through by phone to my wife, but she
is not home. I use my Bell South calling card, one of a few cards that Batelco
will accept. Finally, late in the afternoon I do find my wife at home. I give her
my updated estimate for arrival in the Keys. I tell her I hope to be home in
two weeks, or perhaps a little less, if the weather permits.

On my final trip back to the boat I stop again at the market and buy some
yogurt and coconut ice cream. (I tried the coconut ice cream on the way down
and really liked it.)

Back in the boat I change the engine oil and check over the boat. I suck the
engine oil up from the dipstick tube using my small hand pump and deposit
the oil in a 2-liter water bottle for disposal later. A place here will take my used
engine oil, but I have decided to just bring it home. Everything seems fine with
the boat and engine. I am ready to go in the morning.

It is time now for a drink. I bring out my beach lounge chair and sit on the
back of the boat, watching the traffic go by. Everybody is very friendly. One
dinghy, loaded with eight people, passes by. I wave and simultaneously eight
hands go up. Cruisers are companionable and friendly. I like cruisers.

On another boat, a man climbs the mast.

The ketch next to me belongs to a large family. Several little kids aboard love jumping off the boat into the water. They seem to be traveling in company with another boat, owned by an older couple who I think might be the grand-parents. Dinghies are in constant motion between the two boats. Two other boats near me also seem to be traveling together. A man on the first boat sits on his bow pulpit and talks to a man on the second boat's stern. On another boat, a man climbs the mast.

I am now in the habit of listening to the weather at 6 o'clock on SSB with Perfect Paul. The report has hardly changed over the past week. We still have the high to our north, although I am now getting close to it, and the wind and seas are light. It looks like another day of motorsailing tomorrow.

Finally it is time to eat and I turn on the BBC for entertainment. I have one of my rice dinners. Since starting the trip I have simplified the process of their preparation. I used to cook Minute Rice in my saucepan, and heat the sauce (a can of creamed soup) with the meat in my frying pan. I would then plop the rice on a plate and pour the sauce over the rice. Now I cook the rice, then after the rice sits for its required 5 minutes I pour the soup into the pan and mix it up. Then I put in the meat (canned chicken, canned turkey, canned tuna, canned salmon, or canned sardines) in the pan, and stir and heat a little. After that I eat the whole batch right out of the pan. This saves washing a pan and a plate. (I only do this when my wife is not here. She insists on civilized behavior, which does not, I think, include eating out of the cooking pan.) Tonight I have a can of mushroom soup and a can of salmon with my rice. It is very good.

I listen to the Multitrack Alternative, a BBC music show, at 7:30, then the news at 8. After that I turn to the Voice of America for their slant on the news. The BBC and the VOA usually cover slightly different topics in their news. The BBC has a much stronger emphasis on events in third-world countries, probably because so many of those countries were once British colonies.

In the morning I wait until a couple of hours after sunrise to leave. The long trip out of either of the George Town harbors (Stocking Harbour to the northwest and Elizabeth Harbour to the southeast) requires the ability to spot coral heads. So I sit at the back of the boat eating my breakfast very slowly, and watching a dolphin do lazy circles around *Top Cat*.

I suspect that this dolphin is sleeping. I can't imagine any other reason he would be cruising these barren waters. The water here is 8 feet deep with a sand bottom, and I have seen no fish.

After watching the dolphin go around me for a while, I start to time him, and take a few pictures. He moves very slowly for a dolphin. He takes a little over a minute to circle the boat, never more than a boat-length away, and he always takes three breaths. He seems to take the biggest breath off the port bow, and then always takes another breath very soon after that, within 10 seconds, but not at a fixed interval. He takes the third breath a little later, 10 to 20 seconds after the second. He then does about half the circle without a breath. I think he takes breaths when he is close to a particular spot in the water, but they certainly don't occur at precise locations or regular intervals. On some of his

I suspect that this dolphin is sleeping.

circles he cuts very close to the back of the boat, within a foot or so. And he always crosses over, not under, my anchor line in the front.

Eventually, after I have been watching him for a half hour or so, he comes to a stop, and seems to just drift for a moment, then he turns over on his back and does a couple of jumps as if to wake himself up. And he leaves. Show's over.

I haul up my anchor at about 8:30 in the morning in very calm conditions and leave under engine power. I take the standard doglegs through Stocking Harbour and out the northwest or Conch Cay entrance. (These doglegs are definitely standard routes; they are shown on my chart and in each of my Bahamas guides.) I never see any shallow water. With my shallow draft I am sure I could make it out in a shorter route, but this path has less risk, and takes less effort.

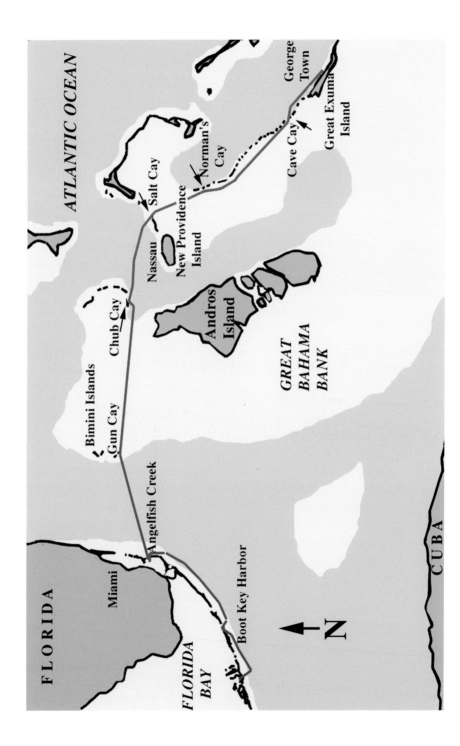

12: The Last Leg

Since I am now legally checked into the Bahamas, I feel like a cruiser again and not just a traveler. I will slow down a little to see more of the Exumas on the way home. This area, together with the Abacos, is said to be the best cruising area in the Bahamas.

Once out in the open water off Conch Cay I put up the sail, but there is practically no wind. The sails will probably add 5 or 10 percent to my speed. The sea is almost calm. There are no other boats. This would be a good day to be going south, with no strong headwind to buck. It is hot today, in the high 90s, and without the wind it feels sweltering. Without the tradewinds nobody would come to these islands.

I arrive at Cave Cut...

The wind never does pick up, but we move steadily forward under power since the sea is so calm. I arrive at Cave Cut at about 3:30. This is a deep and narrow entrance south of Galliot Cut, the cut I used coming down. The rocks and low cliffs on each side of the cut are white and tan, and stand out brightly against the dark sea. A resort is being built on the island on the south side, Musha Cay. A powerboat anchored just inside the cut off Cave Cay is probably waiting for the morning to make the trip to George Town. Though it could start now and get there in two hours, it would then have to enter the harbor in poor light.

A resort is being built on...Musha Cay.

I turn northwest, and immediately *I* am faced with poor light. My chart does not show water depths, but indicates with dotted lines the presence of shallow water. I am soon in water that is 6 feet deep and getting thinner by the minute. I have only a few hundred yards to go until I reach Galliot Cut. From there north I have first-hand experience with the water depths. I slow down and continue parallel to Cave Cay. My depth falls to 5 feet. There are no big heads here, just very shallow water with spotty and small coral growth. Soon the depth increases again, and I look back the way I have come to see in better light that I should have been a little farther off Cave Cay.

I round Galliot Cay and head out to the bank on a course of 260 degrees, following the chart. The water is relatively shallow here, from 6 to 8 feet today, with the tide fairly low, judging from the size of the sandbar visible south of Galliot Cay. I remember this area well from my trip down, and intend to test my theory that it's possible to anchor almost anywhere along Great Guana Cay to the north. This area is all uncharted, mostly uninhabited. The guides show only a couple of places to anchor; these are places near the settlements where cruisers traditionally anchor, places that provide a little more all-weather protection. Once in 10 feet of water, I turn to 330 degrees, roughly paralleling Great Guana Cay.

Otto seems to be having trouble. Every so often he turns the boat sharply to the left. Half the time this results in backwinding the main, which leads to a jibe, and then Otto loses control. I rescue him. I wonder if he is getting sick, or if his fluxgate compass is picking up fields from mineral deposits that my ship's compass seems to miss.

At about 5:30 I head toward a beach on shore. The water depth and bottom have remained very consistent since I first reached the deeper water. The bottom is easily visible in these calm conditions and appears to be sand with a brownish algal growth. There are very occasional grasses, and no coral. I see a small skate and wonder what it eats out here. As I approach shore the water depth remains in the 10- to 12-foot range. The bottom continues to be sand all the way. I pass over what appears to be an inch-wide crack in the sea bottom. I follow it for a bit before losing interest. Perhaps it is a rope.

I stop several hundred yards off shore and anchor. I am a little off the middle of Great Guana Cay, between two cuts. I can be pretty sure of the direction of the tidal current, and doubt it will be strong. The water is glass-clear and dead calm as I lower the anchor. I take a picture of the anchor sitting on a featureless bottom. I set it slowly, and watch as the anchor digs into the sand. Afterward the boat drifts back over the anchor. I listen to the 6 o'clock weather with Perfect Paul and decide I don't need a second anchor tonight.

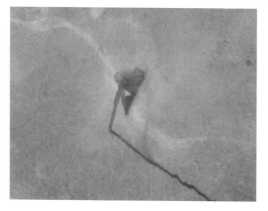

...the anchor sitting on a featureless bottom...

...I claim the island for my very own.

I dinghy to the beach with my drink for a walk. I see no evidence that man has ever been here before, so I claim the island for my very own. I start up the hill for a look around. I am joined by a noisy little bird that flits along beside me. I have a good view from the hill of the interior of the island, which is full of the dwarf palm trees that line the shore.

My bird friend and I head back down the hill and up toward the cape. He leads the way, staying always just ahead of me. Very little flotsam and jetsam litters this beach. I spot only one bottle. I find an old bird nest at the cape, a large nest, constructed with pieces of colorful rope. I climb over the rocks on the cape, and each time I move my little bird friend moves ahead of me. Finally I head back, and again the bird leads the way. Maybe this friendly act is

...a noisy little bird that flits along beside me.

just a ploy to lead me away from a nest but if so, this bird has no concept of direction or, in fact, the actual location of its nest. Or perhaps this is a lonely bird that enjoys human companionship or a curious bird that wonders what I am up to. I say goodbye and get back into my dinghy and leave. Later, I find this bird in my bird guide, I think — a Wilson's plover.

Tonight's supper is rice, pea soup, and a can of chicken. It is a very tasty concoction. I never knew I was such a talented cook. (Or perhaps these weeks of meals from cans and boxes have destroyed my sense of taste.)

In the morning, there is wind, and the day is cooler. I set out under sail, following a 330-degree course up the Exumas, with 10 knots of tailwind. I need to go around the ends of several spits along my path, so I program their coordinates into Geeps Junior. My course appears to pass them all to the west — I will let Junior rest until I get really close to my destination. I see only one

...a beautiful Bahamian sailboat.

other boats out here, a beautiful Bahamian sailboat. It passes quite close to me, a sturdy wooden boat with a gaff rig, obviously making good time.

I begin to see storms to the north. I watch them move, noting their bearing relative to my position using my binoculars, which has a built-in compass. I shift a little toward the west to avoid them.

After lunch and I see no hope of avoiding an approaching thunderstorm. The best I can do is meet it as far to the west as possible, since all the storms seem to be moving east. I pull in the jib and lower the main. I have begun to expect the worst.

The storm hits, and now I have a 25 knot wind out of the northwest, exactly the direction I am going. Is this only coincidence?

Weather truly can turn on a dime at sea. One moment I am running with 10 knots of tailwind, and the next I have a 25-knot headwind! I experience no intervening transitional moments, no gentle cautionary *Are you all ready for this?* And the waves shift almost as quickly. I had rollers coming in from my stern and now I am battling waves breaking over my bow! It is raining, but not hard. I have an engine on but my speed is only half a knot. Waves are regularly crashing over my front windows and the air around me is filled with salt spray. I turn the second engine on and increase the speed to 3 knots. The wind is 27 knots now. After this is over I need a rain without spray to clean *Top Cat* off. I am glad I brought the sails down.

Even with the rain and the waves I can see shoal water to starboard. I keep well to the west of it. The wind shifts to the north, and slows to 20 knots, and then it is 24 knots out of the east. I could sail with this wind, but it is a bit strong. It is hard to make headway. Waves are going in every direction. Now the white-caps are out of the east.

I turn on Geeps Junior for a GPS reading, and he declares he is low on battery power. I bought two sets of spare batteries for Junior in George Town, so I am all set for this.

The wind slacks off. I put up the sails, and sail with a 17-knot wind from the east. Now I am making good time. I am going much faster than I could ever go under power.

As I approach Normans Cay, my destination for the night, I begin to see boats. There are people out here! I was wondering where all the cruisers were. Now

There are people out here!

that I am closer I see only one sailboat. The rest are powerboats, probably on a short trip out of Nassau.

Normans Cay has quite a history. It was a base for a Colombian drug runner for a time. He apparently used the entire island, some four miles long. The bay down the middle of Normans Cay is well protected, and provides a good landing area for seaplanes, and there is an airstrip on the island as well. One plane didn't quite make it; its wreckage is an unusual tourist attraction in the harbor. I am astonished that a crook could pick a place like this, a prime area for cruisers, as a base for drug running. He was guaranteed to have unwanted visitors!

I first visit the downed airplane...

I lower my dinghy into the sea and putter off to see the sights. I first visit the downed airplane, then the remains of a house on the south end of the island. The north end has a resort and a bar. I talk to some boaters who have visited the north end, and they warn me about the voracious mosquitoes (unnecessarily; I have already made their acquaintance). The house on the hill on the south end of the island has a great view, but it is a total wreck. A large radio mast towers over the south end of the island. — A drug lord needs good communications. A public relations firm could make something of this island's notorious past, I think, using the drug-running connection like many other places use pirate history, to give the resort and bar and the beautiful setting some pizzazz.

This area has more small islands and interesting protected waters than any of the other places I have visited so far. I could spend a week exploring. The colors in the water cover the full range, from bright white in the shallows to mid-range turquoises to indigo deeps. I land on several islands. They all have good beaches, but small ones. Most of the islands have extensive rocky shores; I encounter quite a bit of shoal water in my dinghy. The beaches on the east side of the bay are effectively unreachable since the water is so shallow. The east side is lined with mangroves. It reminds me a little of the Keys. But past those islands to the east is another whole line of little islands, and they have beaches that are much easier to reach. Farther to the north is a second Normans Cay anchorage. The entry there is from Exuma Sound, not the Bank. This is a fabulous spot, and I rate it right next to Allan's Cay, just a few miles to the north, also a beautiful and interesting place.

...then the remains of a house on the south end of the island.

I leave in the morning several hours after sunrise for Nassau. There is good light, and I can easily see the shallow areas to the south and west of Normans Cay. The wind is light, 5 to 10 knots out of the south. I put up the sails anyway. The assist from the wind will cut my gas bill in half for this trip.

It is clear that I am back into the world of the megayachts. These boats seem concentrated to the north and south of Nassau. They don't seem to make it south to George Town or west to Bimini. Their wealthy owners probably don't have the time to go that far. Got to get back to work and make the money so they can pay for the upkeep of their expensive boats.

The only risky part of this passage is through the northeast part of Yellow Bank and western part of Middle Ground. There are some heads here, and I see a few. But now I believe they are probably all deeper than my 3 1/2-foot draft. There is one in my path; although I believe it is too deep to give me any grief, I carefully drive around it anyway.

Here I am, in the middle of the crossing, and a storm lies directly in my way! I have been watching storms off to the north all morning, but this one is right here, right now. I close all the hatches and pull in the jib. The jib is not helping much anyway, and now I have less sail out and I can see better. I get no rain, but my wind shifts to the northeast, at 10 knots. This is good. After a bit, I pull out the jib and increase speed by about half.

Yet another boat is bearing down on me. *Collision alert!* It is a sailboat, and I have plenty of time to avoid a close encounter, if it comes to that. I am on a port tack, he is on a starboard tack. It is my responsibility to turn. I turn to the port, and miss him by a few boat lengths. I might have missed him without turning, but it would only have been by a foot or two. Why does this keep happening? What are the chances of so many near-misses on one trip?

I have been suffering for the last two days from hives, but today it is far worse. At first I thought it was from the heat. It has been in the 90s, with little wind — hot and sticky. Now I think I am having a reaction to the penicillin pills. In any case, my midsection is covered with hives. This now bothers me quite a bit more than my arm, which has healed well and is scabbed over nicely.

In an hour or so the wind dies, and I pull in the flapping sails. I sit on the hardtop above the helm, watching for heads with no sails in the way. I can see the instruments well from here, and can reach the engine controls quickly if needed. I take over from Otto, who is still having his problem about turning left, and drive with my feet.

I have not been using Geeps Junior much. Every couple of hours I take a reading to be sure I am where I think I am. By now I feel I pretty much know this area, and I have to watch for heads anyway. So I steer a compass course, and correct the compass course based on landmarks and on what I see in the water. I pass between Yellow Bank and Middle Ground, move to a point off

Rose Island south of the salt pond entrance and east of East Porgy Rock, then head directly north to Rose Island. There are no heads here. I travel west along Rose Island past Rose Rocks to Salt Cay, then wide around the shoals at the east end of Salt Cay, and then finally to my anchorage near the west end of the island. I prefer to track landmarks and watch the water when I can, instead of steering to a set of GPS headings extracted from a chart that is based on very old data. My choice, and so far it has been a successful one.

As I approach the anchorage, it begins to rain. This is good, something to cool off in. But the line of rain moves swiftly over, then seems to retreat back to the north. I watch the rain falling just a hundred yards north of us. It does not return. I am disappointed.

I anchor in about 23 feet of crystal-clear water not far from the rocky shore of Salt Cay. I am in the area labeled on my chart as the Salt Cay Anchorage. One of my guidebooks shows this anchorage, but with a little less water. To the east of me, according to my chart, is some coral. I am reluctant to move closer to shore, but wish I were not in such deep water. Being at the west end of the cay will save me a little time in getting underway tomorrow. The other advantage is that I can easily dinghy to Nassau, and there are no hazards around here. I can see everything on the bottom. It is mainly sand with some grass.

I let out more anchor line than I need, and drive the boat to the south, and drop the second anchor. This one should keep me off the rocks if a strong south wind develops. I pull in some line on my first anchor, still leaving it with a scope of over five I see many enthusiastic tourists. Jetskiers circle. The

I see many enthusiastic tourists.

parasailors are up and soaring. Little runabouts are everywhere. I am not far from Paradise Island beach and its huge hotel, presently under construction. The beach is full of people and little boats. And this is the off season.

The next morning I lock the boat and dinghy over to visit the big city. It is a 15-minute ride. I pass several marinas, then head under the Paradise Island bridge. The traffic is slow over the bridge, but a second bridge is being built, which may account for the traffic jam. I watch a giant crane being moved into place. I continue down the waterfront looking for dinghy docks. I find one at the Bahamas Air-Sea Rescue Association (BASRA) headquarters, but there are no dinghies at their dock, and the dock does not seem low enough to make getting in and out of a dinghy convenient there. (Besides, I still feel a little guilty about not belonging to BASRA.) I stop short of the dock meant for the

I watch a giant crane being moved into place.

big cruise ships. I turn back and stop at one of the marinas. They don't have much of a dinghy dock, but say that I can tie up there. Apparently there is not a strong call for dinghy docks in Nassau. I lock the dinghy as well as I can and start walking.

It is a perilous trip since this is a main road through Nassau...

I locate Shirley Street and head for the Princess Margaret Hospital. It is a perilous trip since this is a main road through Nassau, and it has no shoulder; the sidewalk comes and goes. When the sidewalk is missing I am within inches of the traffic on this two-lane, one-way street.

I finally reach the hospital, which is crowded. I start by waiting in the outpatient line. Eventually I get to the head of the line, and they understand what I need. I give them $5 and they give me a number and very general directions: "through the double doors on your right, then through the next double doors on your left, and to the end of the corridor."

I wander off down the halls looking for the right place. I arrive at what I think is the right place and ask the patients waiting there for advice. One has the same number as I do. That convinces them I am in the wrong place and they set me off on a new route. I follow their advice, through more double doors, but when I get to the new destination, the people there send me on to yet another location. Finally I arrive in an area dedicated to dressing wounds, and they give me a new number. Now I wait with about thirty others.

After about an hour I am ushered into the stitch-removal nurse. She looks at my wound and calls in a doctor. "Isn't it too soon to remove these stitches?" she asks him. He suggests taking out half the stitches, then having me come back in a few days to take care of the rest. I reply that I will not be back here, and that I will be sailing for the next week. He suggests that she take a few stitches out and see how it goes after that. He returns to his work. It appears the decisions are hers. She was just asking for his advice. She takes them all out, and bandages my arm. She tells me not to get the wound wet, not to bump it, and not to stress the arm in any way for the next week. In three days I should have the bandage changed again. I thank her and head back to the boat. Along the way I stop at a Korean market and buy sandwich meat and tomatoes at ridiculously high prices.

I am thankful to find the dinghy still at the dock, undisturbed. I have a great fear of crime in big cities because all the guides warn that that is where most dinghy thefts occur. On my way out I pick up 10 gallons of gas at the marina fuel dock. Now I am back to a full load of gas, and have enough to motor home if there is no wind.

I am grateful to be back in my dinghy, headed back to *Top Cat*, my supplies replenished and the wound looked after. I slow down several times on my way back to take pictures of boats. The police come up once, and say good morning, but don't ask for my identification. I continue on.

I reach the boat late, a little after 11 o'clock. I decide I still can make Chub Cay if I get going right away. I pull the dinghy up on the davits and start pulling in the second anchor. But the two anchor lines have crossed, making it very difficult to pull in the anchor. There was no wind last night, and so of course the boat moved all around in response to tidal currents. I try to turn the boat to unwind the anchors, but eventually give up. The tide is strong right now, and the anchors appear to be well set. I go back to trying to pull in the second anchor, and with the use of both arms I eventually succeed. I am now pretty tired, but begin to pull in the primary anchor. It appears to be hopelessly stuck. How can this be?

I put the dinghy back down and pull it around to the front of the boat, and stick my head in the water with my facemask on. There is wreckage of some sort (the remains of an old car?) directly below, and the anchor chain and anchor are entangled in it. This is not good, I think. I hope I can dislodge it.

Back in the boat I drive the boat to port, to starboard, this way and that, trying to jiggle the anchor loose. I cannot budge it. Having already stressed my arm by pulling on the anchors, I decide to violate the nurse's second rule, not to get the wound wet. I dive on the anchor. I look for something to wrap my arm with, to keep my bandage dry. Good, a plastic bag. I inflate it a little with air and wrap it tightly about my upper arm with tape.

I dive on the anchor. It is very tough just to get down to 23 feet. I look around a bit, and see the junk that has entrapped my anchor. It is steel and iron, but it reaches no more than a couple of feet off the sea floor. It could be a car frame, but there certainly is no cab. This has been here for a while, since a small reef has started to form. I see a sea fan, several sponges, and some red coral. There are also reef fish. Very pretty. The entire junk pile covers the area the size of a car and seems to blend in well with the sand and grasses in front of it.

It looks like a large suspension system is over the chain. This is not going to be easy. I will need my gloves. I could also really use my air compressor, but it didn't work the last time out. I may be able to fix it, but first I will try to move the thing without it. Maybe it will be easier than it appears.

Back in the boat I remove the plastic bag, which has leaked a little, and tape a thick freezer bag in its place. I cut off the top and the bottom, and the bag fits well over the bandage. I have no real hope my bandage will stay dry, but at least I've made the effort.

I put on my gloves and dive again. I make many dives. I cannot understand how the anchor and chain got so ensnared. I try to move things around a bit, but it is tough. I have only a few seconds at the bottom 23 feet down before I must surface for a breath. I do make some progress. I have the anchor moved to a place on one side of the big suspension system and part of the chain untangled. I try repeatedly, but can't lift the suspension system. If somehow I can get the anchor under that big bar I will free it! I try a few more times but I can't seem to do it. The hole doesn't seem quite big enough. And I also worry that I might get the anchor stuck half way through.

The water is becoming much murkier, and now I can barely see the bottom as I snorkel on the surface. I wonder if I should wait for better conditions, like clearer water and less current. But I am not good at waiting. I am really exhausted. How did the anchor and chain get like this? Why did I ever anchor in such deep water? Why are there the remains of a car here? I soon give up fruitless ruminating. The answers to all my questions lie in the past, and the remedy for the problem I have now awaits in the future.

I decide the only thing to do is to disconnect the chain from the rode on the boat and pull the chain through the hole. This surely will work! With enthusiasm, and not much forethought, I get back into *Top Cat* and lower the second anchor to hold the boat while I disconnect the chain and rescue the first anchor.

Back in the water I survey where the second anchor has landed and make sure it is firmly stuck. I snorkel around the area a bit to see what else is here. I count about a dozen junked car frames, all directly below my boat, and all without the cabs. None of them are more than a foot or two off the bottom, making them very hard to see from above. Coral is growing on every surface of these wrecks. Reef fish surround them. How could I have missed this last night? I guess I was looking at the bottom ahead of the junked cars when I chose this place to anchor.

I now realize my second anchor is too close to this junk. I snorkel to the south and east and find a spot with no junked cars. I get back into *Top Cat* and pull the anchor up. Then I get into the dinghy, lower the anchor into the dinghy, and drive off to the full length of my anchor line, 250 feet. I stick my head in the water again with my facemask on, and see just sand and grass, no junked car frames. I drop the anchor. There. I go back to *Top Cat* and pull in as much anchor rode as I can, then tie it off. No backing down on this anchor now.

I return to my trapped anchor. I dive on it and connect a line to it. Then back to *Top Cat* to pull the line as tight as possible. I don't want the boat to drift off when the anchor chain is disconnected.

I detach the anchor chain and drop it into the water. Instantly I realize I have made a mistake. I should have tied a line to it. I need to move this chain to the east side of the junk. Can I do it? I dive on the chain, and try, but the best I can do is to bring it to the surface. The weight of the chain and the strength of the current going west make moving the chain by hand impossible. I temporarily tie the end of the chain to a line on the boat. Then I get into the dinghy and try to pull the chain east over the junk. For some reason I can make no progress.

I anchor the dinghy as far east as I can. Then I get back into *Top Cat* and find my big red anchoring buoy. I will use it to help move the chain..

I get back in the water and tie the end of the chain to the big red buoy, and try to move it over the junk as I snorkel along. In this way, I guide the chain over the junk without getting it hung up. I work at this for half an hour, and make some progress. The chain is heavy, and the current is strong. If I could guide the chain while someone pulls me in the dinghy this process would be easy. But alone as I am, I cannot see and drive at the same time, and I probably am pulling the chain into areas I shouldn't. After a while I conclude that I have done the best I can and I drop the chain. I have the last twenty feet of the chain on the east side of the junk, but I can see that part of the first 20 feet of chain is stuck on something in the junk. I return to the boat to get my gloves. With the gloves on I dive on the chain and move it to the other section. I am exhausted as I return to attempt to pull up the anchor, this time anchor-first, the chain trailing along behind.

Back on the boat I pull with both arms. Soon I have the anchor up near the boat and the 40 feet of chain under it. The chain weighs more than the anchor. I am not strong enough to pull this lot aboard. To do it I have to reach over the side and pull it straight up. I can't pull it over the anchor roller upside down. I go back in the dinghy, and grab the chain. I pull the chain up link by link into the dinghy, then I pull up the safety line I attached to the end of the chain. That's it, it's all out of the water now.

I climb aboard *Top Cat* and pull the chain on the dinghy aboard. Now I can easily pull up the 35-pound anchor. Once this is done I set the second anchor. I do not have the energy to dive on it.

An unenlightened reader, one without a driving need for adventure, may ask at this juncture: why didn't I abandon the anchor? (After all I do have two others.) Or why didn't I seek help in retrieving it? This misses much of the point of my trip, which is to successfully meet small challenges like stuck an-chors and to do it *alone*. After the event I felt very good about my success in retrieving the anchor. And I would never leave my anchor. I cherish my big 35-pound anchor and its 40-foot chain. This is the best anchor and chain I have ever had.

I spend the next half hour putting everything back, and taking a freshwater shower. It is now 4:30, far too late to try for Chub Cay, and my bandage is soaked. I must change it. I have no bandages that are big enough on the boat, but I can use two small ones. I also have no bandage wrap, so I will reuse the wet one. I take the bandage wrap off and hang it out to dry on the lifeline. I bathe my wound in hydrogen peroxide, one of the really useful items I have in my first aid bag. I now see why my nurses have been so insistent in telling me not to use the arm. The wound is not completely closed. But the gap is much less than on the first day.

Once my bandage is changed, and everything has been put away, I decide to set out on a dinghy ride to Paradise Island. There is still no wind, and the fast dinghy ride will cool me off.

Within five minutes I am among tourists. There are dozens of people on the beach, but I watch those on the water. There are several people being pulled by boats into the air, the parasailors. Most go up in tandem rigs, two at a time. There are skiers, including one real athlete who is doing 360-degree turns. I see some small sailboats. One group of about ten tourists is pulled past me in a long yellow float. Most of the noise comes from the jetskiers. Many of these seem to be locals.

My chart shows a canal that cuts through Paradise Island and I go looking for it. I find it, right in front of the new hotel, and dinghy in. It ends at the new hotel, but there is quite a bit of construction on its edges, and it probably did at one time go through to the harbor. The hotel looks like something built by Disney, sparing no expense to achieve a state of near-perfection. The sugar sand looks imported. The large and healthy palms seem to have been placed for maximum glamor. A protected lagoon is going in right in front of the hotel. I drive around the inside lagoon, sharing it with a man and his son peddling along on a paddleboat. On my way out I pass a four-foot barracuda. I reflect that the barracuda will elicit many excited exclamations from swimming tourists in the future.

Early the next morning I pull up the anchor without problem, and head out toward Chub Cay. It is windless, and the water is again transparent. I make a slight detour to look at the junked cars. I pass right over them. They really do blend in well with the little clumps of grass in that area. I suppose it is possible that I looked right at them when I dropped the anchor, seeing nothing at all.

My experience with anchoring last night underscores the importance of diving on the anchor and of anchoring in water shallow enough so I can reach

The hotel looks like something built by Disney...

the anchor easily in snorkel gear. I was unable to dive on the anchor when I set it, which probably would have allowed me to detect the junk and move on to another spot before I became entangled. I was too eager to anchor instead of taking the time to find the best place.

I motor out with my sails down in dead calm water, passing three large cruise ships lined up to enter Nassau Harbor. They all appear to be dead in the water. They gray morning mist and the gray water merge, and the ships seem to float in the air. I am overflown by a USCG helicopter, so low that I am sure it could hit my mast with a slight change in course. I suppose the Coast Guards personnel aboard can use binoculars to read the boat name, and perhaps even my Florida registration number, to identify me.

By 10 o'clock the wind picks up a little, so I raise the sail. This allows me to reduce my engine speed somewhat and save my gas. I am on target for arrival at Chub Cay around 3.

...the ships seem to float in the air.

As I near Chub Cay I am joined by about 20 dolphins, the largest group I have ever seen from *Top Cat*. As dolphins go, these are small ones, only about 3 to 4 feet long. They are very athletic, like all dolphins, and continually pass each other as they cross at the bow of the boat. They go much faster than *Top Cat*, making great circles around the boat, then surging well ahead. Holding onto the jib stay, I stand in the center of the bow. These are beautiful animals. They have distinctive streaks of grayish-white on their heads. The water is so clear I can see them perfectly, even when they dive deep. After about 15 minutes they lose interest and leave.

...I am joined by...dolphins...

I turn up past Chub Point and join four other sailboats in the anchorage. I go much closer to the beach than the others, and anchor in seven feet of water. Low tide is not until 8 o'clock tonight, according to my almanac; I have arrived near the time of high tide. But the tidal range is only a couple of feet here. I put out two anchors, about 180 degrees apart, anticipating a change in the direction of tide after the wind dies. The other boats are not within swinging distance of me, and at least one of those boats has two anchors out as well.

Once the anchors are set I head out in the dinghy to do a little exploring. I motor down the mile-long Mama Rhoda Channel between Chub Cay and Mama Rhoda Cay. This channel has only a few feet of water and fast-moving current. The water varies in color from brilliant white to very dark, indicating a variety of bottom conditions. I see four or five rays before I reach the end of the channel. They stand out starkly against the white sand in the middle of the channel. As I approach they hustle to the darker water along the edges. That water is about the same depth, but the bottom is grass and once the ray reaches the dark background of grass it disappears from view.

...a shark...in water so clear it seems to be trapped under glass

I stop at a little spit at the far end of the channel and watch a shark swimming in the shallows, in water so clear that it seems to be trapped under glass. The spit points to the north, to the Grand Bahama Bank and the chain of Berry Islands. Chub Cay, one of the Berry Islands, is at the extreme southwestern end of the chain. The banks to the north are quite shallow, and impenetrable in many areas except by dinghy.

I make stops at a few more beaches. Then I head back, and into the Chub Cay Club marina. The entrance channel seems shallow, perhaps four or five feet. But inside the water is very murky, and I can't see the bottom to estimate the depth. There are sailboats here, and many large powerboats, mostly sportfishing boats. This is a private club. I see club members moving about on golf carts and bicycles. There is an airport here, and a fine beach.

A powerboater on a 39-foot Sea Ray moves in close to the beach and in front of me. He has been working on anchoring the boat for some time, putting out two small Danforth anchors, and diving on them repeatedly. His boat keeps swinging back and forth through very large angles, and is rolling severely. This may be troubling him, or he perhaps he has no confidence that his tiny anchors will hold tonight and wants to set them as securely as possible. This worries me, because if he drags his anchors, his boat could drift into mine. Boats of this kind (with worried captains) usually end up in marinas.

Before supper several more sailboats have made their way into this small anchorage. This is a popular spot, the only good place to anchor between here and Gun Cay on the west side of the Bahama Bank. It is clearly the anchorage of choice for boats crossing the Bank to Nassau. I now have another neighbor, but this one is in deeper water. I am in only 5 feet of water. Many boats can't anchor in water this shallow so I am often off by myself in shallow areas.

I get up in the dark at 3:15 to get underway for the long trip over the Bank. This time I want to avoid anchoring on it overnight. It is a pitch-black night, no moon, no stars. For a moment or two I have second thoughts about leaving on such a dark night, since I cannot see the boats that have not turned on their anchor lights. The few sailboats that have anchor lights have them at the top of their masts. I much prefer a light lower on the boat (I have both), since it is easier to see at close range, where there is the danger of collision. Although I don't see the boats well, the Chub Point light is working, and shows me where the land is. I think I remember where the boats are. — And I have a flashlight. That, I tell myself, will at least provide reassurance if I hear or see something that makes me think I'm nearing another boat.

I begin the long chore of bringing up two heavy anchors. This takes me some time, but is relatively easy since the wind is light and the current was insufficient this night to swing the boat around. *Top Cat's* orientation is as it was when I went to bed. I let the primary anchor line out, then retrieve the second anchor. Then I retrieve the primary anchor.

I motor out of the anchorage watching for anchored boats very carefully. It seems to take forever to finally make it to deep water. By the time I am out at ocean depths it is well past 4 o'clock and I already feel I am falling behind schedule. There is very little wind, so I continue to motor. My hope is to arrive at the Northwest Channel light at sunrise. Without supporting wind I soon lose all chance. Eventually I arrive, about an hour after sunrise. I didn't want to arrive in the dark, since I could run into the Channel light. When I arrive, however, there is plenty of daylight. The light looks even worse than I remember. It was hit by a boat some years ago, or perhaps several boats, no doubt trying to cross the Bank on some dark and moonless night, and it is a listing, rusting wreck.

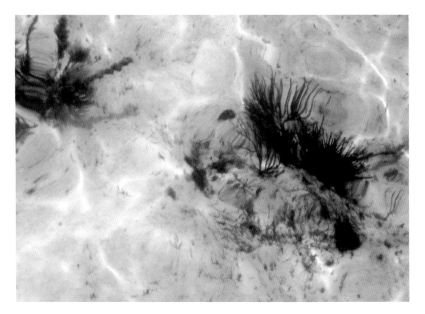

Every so often I reach an oasis, an area with some growth.

Several powerboats pass me soon after I reach the Bank. After that I am alone. For much of this trip I see nothing on the sea bottom. The water is clear and the bottom appears devoid of plant or animal life. It looks like one large swimming pool. Every so often I reach an oasis, an area with some growth. I see no big coral heads. Instead, there are barrel sponges, sea fans, sea grasses, and pillar corals. It seems to me one would have to be pretty unlucky to hit a head on this route between the Northwest Channel light and Cat Cay. On the other hand, I remember the large number of collisions I have avoided while on this trip. I will be cautious.

I arrive at Cat Cay on schedule at about 6:30. I continue to motorsail up past the Gun Cay cut, and anchor east of Gun Cay, not far from Honeymoon Harbor. Several other sailboats have anchored here before me, but none are closer than a hundred yards.

I dinghy over to Honeymoon Harbor to see how it has changed since I visited at the start of this trip. A number of powerboats are here, and a few sailboats. Traffic between Honeymoon Harbor and South Florida is always heavy. The wreckage of the beached boat that was conspicuous several months ago has almost disappeared. There must have been some rough weather here since my last visit.

I check the weather on VHF WX-1 out of Miami. The forecast is for light winds for the next several days. I suppose I will motorsail the rest of the way.

I leave in the morning to cross a calm Gulf Stream, beginning a three-day trip home. Early in the afternoon I begin to smell smoke. The smell gets stronger and stronger. Is something on fire? I explore the boat, looking for smoke, and then I spot a freighter on the horizon, only a speck, but a speck with a plume of smoke hanging over it. It's the freighter I smell, not something on my boat.

The winds are light and the sea is almost flat, but because of the 3-knot current, the trip is slow. I try to go across the Stream as directly as I can. I will head south when I get out of the current. This strategy results in a greater distance traveled.

Once I am through the Stream, my speed, as calculated by GPS updates, picks up rapidly. Since the sea is so calm there is no big advantage going down on the inside, behind the line of reefs. I will stay in the deep ocean for the rest of my journey. I travel south on the outside of the reef line, a more direct route to Angelfish Creek. I pass through the creek and anchor in Card Sound for the night. Then I am up early for the trip down Hawk Channel, intending to stop as I usually do in Long Key Bight. But I get to Long Key Bight so early, motoring all the way, that I decide to go a little further to Boot Key Harbor, in Marathon, where many cruisers hang out. On my way in, I pass West Sister Rock, a popular place for boaters, and crowded today.

I arrive at Marathon a little late with a calm sea. I anchor out, since the weather is predicted to be very calm, and I plan a quick start in the morning. I dinghy in to Boot Key Harbor to take a look at the cruisers. The harbor is crowded,

...West Sister Rock, a popular place for boaters, and crowded today.

as usual. This is one of the most popular places for cruisers in the Keys. It has a long history as an anchorage. Many of the people here live aboard their boats and never leave the harbor, as evidenced by the shaggy condition of their anchor rodes. I ride through past scores of cruiser boats. I see a few cruisers out on their decks, working or relaxing, and I imagine that they are quite satisfied with their lives. In this quiet and beautiful harbor the idea of living on a boat and cruising the clear waters between here and South American seems inviting.

...Boot Key Harbor...

In the morning I wake at 4:30. I want to make sure I reach the channel that goes to *Top Cat's* home canal within a few hours of the morning's high tide. I am convinced from personal experience that most accidents happen close to home. Almost all the times I have hit bottom have been in the channel near home. I reach the channel about 10 o'clock and in the shallowest stretch, only a few inches of water lie under my keel.

As I pull into my canal I feel very happy about completing this trip. I will miss the adventure of the sea, the challenge of finding my way from place to place and supplying my needs aboard the little world of my boat, but I am glad to be home.

Afterword

I have had a very successful trip. I have had a good time. I have also clarified in my mind my interest in the cruising life.

I have met many different cruising couples. Each has a distinctive style. Some cruisers sail alone, while some sail in company with cruisers in other boats. Some do it all year, some only part of the year. Some travel a lot, while others stay put in one beautiful and convenient spot. Some work part of the year. Others never work. Most, I think, are in their late fifties. Some are in their sixties. A few are in their seventies, and I met one in his eighties. Most have all their money in their boat. Some have enough money for a house as well.

Cruising is most often a life for couples, although some cruise with their children and a few hardy adventurers travel alone. A solo cruiser doesn't fit in well with the cruising community. I certainly missed my wife on the trip to and from the Virgin Islands. I'd like to share my experiences in real time, and I have had no one to share them with.

There are definitely ups and downs in cruising. Sometimes I have been bored, other times anxious. Cruising is not dangerous if travel is limited to relatively good weather, and is planned out thoroughly. At times cruising is exhilarating. I particularly enjoy a first visit to a small, uninhabited island or walking a lovely beach for the first time. There is a special peacefulness about sailing in good weather. I have found a very strong sense of community among cruisers. They tend to be a very friendly group. Most of the cruisers I have talked to do the Caribbean circuit, and continually renew friendships from previous trips. I find I enjoy the traveling much more than the socializing.

To me the choice is between traveling most of the time and seeing very different places or sailing only part of the year, and staying in a house the rest of the time. Right now, the second option appeals to me most but that may change as the years pass and fewer interests and responsibilities bind me to the land.

Index

Visit the Tortuga Books web site at

www.tortugabooks.com

To order additional copies of

Sailing Through Paradise
The Illustrated Adventures of
a Single-handed Sailor

send $24.95* plus $4.00 shipping and
handling to

Tortuga Books
Box 420564
Summerland Key, FL 33042

*Florida residents add 6% state sales tax plus your county
surtax.